PROCESS OF CONSCIOUSNESS
AND
MATTER

PROCESS OF CONSCIOUSNESS AND MATTER

This book is intended for all serious students of the Abhidhamma. It serves as supplement to Bhikku Bodhi's book *A Comprehensive Manual of Abhidhamma*, and treats various important aspects in more detail - in particular the process of consciousness and matter.

by
(Aggamahāpaṇḍita)
Bhaddanta Dr. Rewata Dhamma

Edited by
(Aggamahāpaṇḍita)
Ven. Dr. Kumarabhivamsa

2004

Pariyatti Press
an imprint of

Pariyatti Publishing
867 Larmon Road, Onalaska, WA, USA 98570

www.pariyatti.org

With thanks to Birmingham Buddhist Vihara for giving permission for *Process of Consciousness and Matter* to be republished, and to Triple Gem Publications for creating the print-ready manuscript.

First Pariyatti Press Edition – 2015

ISBN: 978-1-938754-62-3 (softcover)
978-1-938754-65-4 (PDF ebook)
978-1-938754-66-1 (ePub)
978-1-938754-67-8 (Mobi)

Library of Congress Control Number: 2014909029

Cover designed by Daniel Haskett

CONTENTS

CHAPTER I
CONSCIOUSNESS AND ITS FACTORS

CHAPTER II
PROCESS OF CONSCIOUSNESS
(CITTA VĪTHI)

CHAPTER III
MIND-DOOR COGNITIVE PROCESS
(MANODVĀRA VĪTHI)

CHAPTER IV
ABSORPTION JAVANA IN THE MIND-DOOR PROCESS
(APPANĀ JAVANAVĀRA MANODVĀRA VĪTHI)

CHAPTER V
PROCESS OF MATTER

LIST OF TABLES

CHAPTER I

1.1 The 52 Mental Factors at a Glance

CHAPTER II

2.1 The Process with an Object of a Very Great Intensity
2.2 Five-Door Cognitive Process
2.3 The Cognitive Process of Eye-Door without Transitional Bhavanga
2.4 The Cognitive Process of Eye-Door with Transitional Bhavanga
2.5 First Cognitive Process with a Great Object at the Eye-Door without Transitional Bhavanga
2.6 First Cognitive Process with a Great Object at the Eye-Door with Transitional Bhavanga
2.7 The Process with a Slight Object at the Eye-door
2.8 The Process with a Very Slight Object at the Eye-door

CHAPTER III

3.1 Cognitive Process with a Clear Object Ending at the Registration
3.2 The Process Ending with Javana
3.3 The Cognitive Process with Other Objects
3.4 The Cognitive Process in Dream State

CHAPTER IV

4.1 Dull-Witted Beginner's Jhānic Process
4.2 Keen-Witted Beginner's Jhānic Process
4.3 Entering Jhānic Absorption Process
4.4 Dull-Witted First Jhāna Stream Enterer Path Process
4.5 Keen-Witted First Jhāna Stream Enterer Path Process
4.6 Dull-Witted First Jhāna Higher Path Process
4.7 Keen-Witted First Jhāna Higher Path process
4.8 Dull-Witted Entering First Jhāna Stream Enterer Fruition Process

CHAPTER V

ABBREVIATIONS

NAMES OF TEXTS

AP = Abhidhamma Pakasani
As = Atthasalini
AnA = Anguttara Atthakatha
BS = Basic Sangaha (in Myanmar)
CMA = A Comprehensive Manual of Abhidhamma
Dhp. = Dhammapada
Di = Dighanikaya
DiA = Dighanikaya Atthakatha
MA = Manual of Abhidhamma
PCM = Process of Consciousness and Matter
PD = Paramattha Dipani
PP = The Path of Purification
SbT = Sangaha Bhāsā Tīkā (in Myanmar)
Smv = Sammohavinodanī (Commentary to Vibhaṅga)
Vb = Vibhaṅga
VS = Vīthi & Hso yoe (in Myanmar)
Vism = Visuddhimagga

TERMS USED AND TABLES

Five-Door Cognitive Process

000 = the three minor instants of arising, existing and dissolution of one thought moment
SB = stream of bhavanga
PB = past bhavanga
VB = vibrating bhavanga
AB = arresting bhavanga
Cons = consciousness
FA = five-door adverting
EC = eye consciousness
RC = receiving consciousness
IC = investigating consciousness
DC = determining consciousness
JC = javana consciousness
RS = registration
EC = eye consciousness
HC = hearing consciousness
SC = smelling consciousness
TC = tasting consciousness
BD = body (touching) consciousness

The Cognitive Process with a Very Great Object Ending with Javana

SB = stream of bhavanga
PB = past bhavanga
VB = vibrating bhavanga
AB = arresting bhavanga
FA = five-door adverting
EC = eye consciousness
RC = receiving consciousness
IC = investigating consciousness
DC = determining consciousness
JC = javana consciousness
BC = bhavanga consciousness

RS = registration
TB = transitional (āgantuka) bhavanga
BC = bhavanga consciousness

Mind-Door Cognitive Process
SB = stream of bhavanga
PB = past bhavanga
VB = vibrating bhavanga
AB = arresting bhavanga
MA= mind-door adverting
JC = javana consciousness
RS = registration
BC = bhavanga consciousness

Absorption Javana Process
SB = stream of bhavanga
VB = vibrating bhavanga
AB = arrested bhavanga
MA= mind-door adverting
PR = preparation
AC = access consciousness
CO = conformity
CL = change-of lineage
JH = jhānic citta

The Path Process
MC= the path citta
FC = fruition citta
PF = purification (vodāna)

Entering Attainment of Fruition Process
FJ = fruition javana
.... = fruition javana (as long as)

PREFACE

Whenever I reach the *Abhidhammatthasangaha* (chapter IV), while teaching Abhidhamma, I find myself wishing that there were an English treatise on the Thought Process described there. There are books in the Myanmar language on this subject but they are not accessible to all my students and I have no time to explain since I don't want the Abhidhamma Course to be too long. A book in English would therefore be very good for the students. Then they could read it by themselves and only need explanations from their teacher in some difficult places.

Now my friend in Birmingham, Dr. Rewata Dhamma Aggamahāpaṇḍita, has written *Process of Consciousness and Matter*, the very book I had in mind. He is an expert on Abhidhamma and is also co-author of *A Comprehensive Manual of Abhidhamma*, which has become a textbook on the subject. In this latest book of his he explains in detail all aspects of the thought and matter processes.

The subject is barely covered in the Commentaries and Sub-commentaries, but our Myanmar teachers of old have written detailed treatises drawing on what has been said there and made it a special study. Previously you could not find such studies in any other language than our own. In Myanmar monks have to learn from them in order to be proficient in Abhidhamma. Now that Dr. Rewata Dhamma has written his book in English, any person who can read that language can also thoroughly understand the thought and matter processes.

Dr. Rewata Dhamma's addition to the literature on Abhidhamma thus fulfils a long felt need. In my opinion, his book will be prized alike by students of Abhidhamma and scholars in general as a precious and unique contribution to that literature.

U. Silānanda
Dhammānanda Vihāra
17450 South Cabrillo Hwy
Half Moon Bay CA 94019-2518

ACKNOWLEDGEMENT

After Dr Rewata Dhamma's death, this study of *Process of Consciousness and Matter* was checked and edited Mike Regan, Dr Kumarabhivamsa, Pro-Rector of the International Theravada Buddhist Missionary University, and myself. The readership its author intended was all serious students of Abhidhamma but the book seems to me suitable for anyone interested in the mental process and especially scientists. The subject is deep and touches upon the disciplines of Mathematics, Chemistry and Physics. For clear understanding, however, a basic knowledge of Abhidhamma is necessary, such as can be gained from *A Comprehensive Manual of Abhidhamma*, co-authored by Bhikkhu Bodhi and Dr Rewata Dhamma (Kandy, 1993). Let me further suggest to readers who have difficulty mastering the subject that they ask some learned monk for elucidation – and particularly one from Myanmar whose speciality it is.

My sincere thanks to Aggamahāpaṇḍita Ven.Dr. Silānandā bhivamsa, Rector of the International Theravada Buddhist Missionary University, Yangon, for kindly writing a preface at the author's request. I am also grateful to Aggamahāpaṇḍita Ven.Dr Kumarā bhivamsa, Pro-Rector (ITBMU), Mike Regan and Linda Tomlinson for their thorough work. Also to Robert Black for producing a glossary and index in addition to co-operating in the preparation of the text for printing with U. Tosana (London Buddha Vihara). Finally, I would like to thank U. Tin Htoon, of Triple Gem Publications, for arranging the financing and publishing of this book.

Dr Ottaranyāna
Birmingham Buddhist Vihara
UK

14/05/2007

DR. REWATA DHAMMA

Born in Myanmar in 1929, Ven. Rewata Dhamma studied under several eminent scholar monks from a young age. After completing higher studies, he was given a state scholarship in 1956 to study Hindi and Sanskrit in India. He went on to study Indian philosophy and Mahayana Buddhism, gaining his Ph.D. from Varanasi University in 1967. He edited and published the *Abhidhammattha Sangaha* with its commentary in 1965 and a Hindi translation of this, with his own commentary in Hindi, in 1967. For the latter he received the Kalidasa Prize from the Hindi Academy for one of the outstanding books of the year and it still remains a university textbook in India.

In 1975 he was invited to England, where he eventually set up the West Midlands Buddhist Centre, finally to become the Birmingham Buddhist Vihara. From this base he travelled to Europe, as well as the U.S.A., Mexico and Brazil, teaching Buddhism and leading Insight Meditation retreats in various centres and universities. He was also highly regarded in Asia and served on a number of commissions and international Buddhist bodies. In 2000 the Government of Myanmar awarded him the prestigious title of Aggamahāpaṇḍita.

In 1998 Sayadaw realised his dream of housing the Buddha relics, formerly belonging to the Myanmar royal family, in the Dhammatalaka Peace Pagoda, which opened the same year. Subsequently he opened the Sangharama Monastery on the same site and was planning to build a Buddhist academy there too prior to his death on 26 May, 2004.

Other books by Dr Rewata Dhamma include *A Comprehensive Manual of Abhidhamma* (with Bhikkhu Bodhi, Buddhist Publication Society, Sri Lanka, 1993); *The First Discourse of the Buddha* (Wisdom Publications, USA, 1997); *The Buddha and His Disciples* (Dhammatalaka Publications, UK, 2001); *Emptying the Rose-Apple Seat* (Triple Gem Publications, USA, 2003) and *The Buddha's Prescription* (Triple Gem Publications, USA, 2005).

Venerable Dr. Rewata Dhamma passed away peacefully in his sleep in the early morning of 26th May 2004.

INTRODUCTION

This book is intended for all serious students of the Abhidhamma. It serves as supplement to Bhikku Bodhi's book *A Comprehensive Manual of Abhidhamma*, and treats various important aspects in more detail - in particular the process of consciousness.

All Buddhist teachings, including all the multitude of different schools and approaches, have the same basic aim - to attain liberation. In Buddhism liberation means becoming free from the limited boundaries and the suffering that characterise our samsaric existence. The Buddha taught that we can only realise this liberation by means of our own efforts, directed towards a deep understanding of ourselves and the world around us. We will not realise such an understanding simply by being "handed it on a plate" by someone else, however exalted or even divine that person or being is.

Buddhist teachings may be regarded as having two main strands: conventional teachings and ultimate teachings. The main repository of the Buddha's conventional teachings is the Sutta Pitaka. In these suttas most of the teachings are directed towards ethics, and explain how people caught up in samsara can live their lives in a kinder and more wholesome way. The Buddha knew that many, even most, human beings will not achieve liberation immediately. What they must therefore do is to try and move gradually towards liberation. Depending on their past kamma and their present effort, they may realise liberation in this life, or it may be in their next life, or in some future life.

In the "ultimate" teachings of the Buddha however, as presented in the Abhidhamma Pitaka, we are provided with another perspective. The Abhidhamma talks in a more abstract way than does the Sutta Pitaka. The teachings in the Abhidhamma (which means teachings that are "special" or "supra mundane") define the universe in terms of nāma rūpa, i.e. mental and material phenomena. The aim of the Abhidhamma is to lead us towards a deep understanding of the true nature of ourselves and the world around us. In order to attain final liberation we have to see these truths directly.

In certain respects we can see some similarities between the Abhidhamma and modern Western science. We need to recognise though that the Buddha taught over 2600 years ago, in an Asian culture and tradition. The teachings are therefore presented in a style and format which people of that time and place could most readily assimilate. Looking at the Abhidhamma today we find that there are many concepts and terms for which there are no direct Western equivalents.

The Abhidhamma is not just metaphysics, rather it is a complete psycho-ethical system. Furthermore, the Abhidhamma is not just concerned with spiritual development. It deals in detail with both the human body and the mind, and many commentaries and sub-commentaries have been written by the Buddhist masters of the East about both these subjects. In Myanmar a traditional form of medicine has been developed based on the Abhidhamma. We can see something of a parallel here in the way that Western medicine draws on the more fundamental understanding developed in "basic" subjects such as biology, physics and chemistry.

When the Abhidhamma speaks about the mind it is referring to the combination of two distinct but related phenomena i.e. "consciousness" (citta) and "mental factors" (cetasika). In everyday language when we speak about "the mind" we are generally referring to what the Abhidhamma would more precisely define as the mental factors or cetasika. The Abhidhamma explains that citta and cetasika cannot arise separately, but in fact always "co-exist" with each other. Altogether there are 52 individual cetasikas, each always arising with its accompanying citta. At any given moment several cetasikas may be present in the mind, depending on circumstances. Some of the cetasikas have a purifying effect on the mind, some can defile it, and others are neutral. The overall state of the mind is dependent on how the individual cetasikas combine with each other, and these combinations can result in up to 121 cittas. It is the combination of the cetasikas which makes us sometimes happy, sometimes sad, and sometimes neutral. The cittas and their concomitant cetasikas are continuously arising and passing away, millions of times a second[1]. It is not possible for the mundane mind to understand this ceaseless mental activity.

In Buddhism the mind is very important: "Mind is the forerunner of all activity, mind is chief, all is mind made"[2]. In order to understand the ceaselessly changing nature of the mind one has to develop it in various ways. The Buddha taught two kinds of meditation: concentration or tranquillity (samatha) and insight or understanding (vipassanā). If one practices samatha one's mind becomes pure and concentrated. Only with a concentrated mind can one see things as they truly are, this is the insight of vipassanā. We can here draw an analogy with the modern scientist (say a biologist or physicist), who needs special equipment in order to do his work. Thus a biologist may need a microscope, or a physicist may need a particle accelerator. They need this equipment in order to effectively and systematically study within their respective domains - of organic and inorganic matter. In a similar way the student of the fundamental realities spoken of in the Abhidhamma must have a "tool" and that tool is none other than the student's own highly concentrated mind. To that end the student of the Abhidhamma must make considerable effort to train, develop and purify the mind. This effort must be all encompassing, and the Buddha spoke of three aspects: morality (sīla), concentration (samatha) and wisdom (paññā). Without effort in all these areas it is not possible to attain the final liberation offered by vipassanā.

Mind and Matter

The Abhidhamma deals in detail with all mental and material phenomena and their interdependence. In Western philosophy there is no detailed treatment of consciousness as a separate entity, instead it is spoken of in terms of the way the brain uses consciousness. Even modern Western psychology does not tackle the nature of consciousness itself but instead is limited to the study of behaviour (be it human or animal).

In Buddhism a human being is regarded as being mind and matter and nothing else.Therefore, the Abhidhamma looks at mind and matter in great detail[3]. In fact when we see what we call a "human being", we are really seeing a manifestation of a deeper underlying reality, i.e. that certain mental and material phenomena have combined together. The Abhidhamma enumerates 28 different kinds of matter, and also describes subtle particles known as kalāpas. These subtle particles cannot be seen with the naked eye or felt by touch but one can experience them in the body as qualities or energies.

The Abhidhamma describes how states of consciousness, states of mind and states of matter arise and pass away millions of time each second. One whose mind is developed through the practice of meditation can experience these realities, how they arise and pass away on a moment by moment basis. In fact during each moment the consciousnesses and material elements arise and pass away many millions of times. Someone who does not know about the Abhidhamma will have great difficulty understanding this incredibly rapid process.

To draw another analogy with modern science we could say that if one reads a book on theoretical physics, then one could develop a better understanding of say the structure of the atom. However, to pursue this analogy with science a little further, we must realise that the knowledge of the theoretical physicist is just that, it is only theoretical intellectual knowledge. It is only when the physicist uses the correct equipment (such as a particle accelerator) to directly observe matter, that they will actually have direct experience of the phenomena of the material world that they so wants to understand. A biologist or a biochemist must go to the laboratory and use a microscope or some other equipment, in order to actually see for themselves the microbes and complex molecular structures that they have learned about in the lecture theatre.

In a similar way, if one studies the Abhidhamma, then yes, certainly one's intellectual understanding of the realities that it talks about in such fine detail will certainly deepen. However, it is only by the practice of meditation that these realities can actually be experienced. In this book I am trying to explain the process of consciousness and matter according to the Abhidhamma teachings. I fully appreciate that a reader who does not have some prior knowledge of the language and terminology, in which the Abhidhamma is expressed, will not be able to understand what I have to say. It is rather like someone who has not studied mathematics trying to read a theoretical treatise on quantum mechanics, which is chock full of mathematical equations and abstract terminology that may seriously discourage him. However, it is my hope that if the reader puts in the necessary groundwork and studies the Abhidhamma seriously, their understanding will gradually deepen.

Abhidhamma Studies

Those readers who are Buddhists, or have had at least some prior contact with Buddhism, will know that the Abhidhamma represents a very important (if rather difficult) part of the Buddha's teachings. On the other hand, many people for whom Buddhism is such a tremendous source of inspiration have not actually studied the Abhidhamma and so have not been able to benefit from its wisdom. However, as Buddhism spreads all over the world, I am finding that there is renewed interest in the Abhidhamma. I know many groups in Europe, America and Asia who are now studying the Abhidhamma very enthusiastically.

In the early 1990s Bhikku Bodhi asked me to write a short introduction to his book *A Comprehensive Manual of Abhidhamma*. The book was subsequently published in 1993 by the Buddhist Publication Society of Sri Lanka. He had specifically asked me for only a very brief note, since he knew that my own book on the subject (written in Hindi) was very long, over 1000 pages. Bhikku Bodhi's book was greatly welcomed by Western students of the Abhidhamma, and has been reprinted several times.

One aspect of *A Comprehensive Manual of Abhidhamma* is that it describes the process of consciousness only very briefly, based directly on the rather terse original Pāli scriptural text. Many of my students in Europe have subsequently asked me to write in more detail on this subject, so that their understanding of it may deepen. In the present book I write not only about the process of consciousness but also about material processes, in particular about kalāpas. What I have written is very much based on my original Hindi commentary and also on certain existing Burmese texts. It is very difficult for a student to find this type of material outside Myanmar. Since the 17th century Burmese masters of the Abhidhamma have produced very high quality books and commentaries on the Abhidhamma. It is my belief that it is not possible to understand the Abhidhamma in detail without access to this type of material.

In this book whatever I say about the process of mind and matter is intended to supplement what has already been presented in Bhikku Bodhi's book *A Comprehensive Manual of Abhidhamma.* I recommend that the serious student should read and reread the Manual again and again, in order to become familiar with the technical terminology and language used in this area. I would like to add that I also feel that Chapter 8 of the Manual needs further detail on causal relations, and I intend to write more on this at a later date.

Process of Consciousness

As human beings our sense consciousnesses, occurring at each of our five sense doors, arise and pass away millions of times each second. It needs to be understood that, because there are several sense doors there is not just one process occurring, there are many. Thus, for example, as we sit in meditation we may be experiencing many processes, such as feeling contact with the ground, and also seeing, hearing and so on. However, the sense consciousnesses themselves are not occurring simultaneously, even though it may seem that they are happening in the same mind moment. They seem to be happening simultaneously only because they follow one after the other at such an incredibly rapid rate. Therefore, I first of all explain that the processes arising at the five sense doors arise in respect of their own different respective objects[4]. I then explain how the sense object consciousness arises at each sense door. With regard to the sixth sense door, the mind, I explain that the mind door process is a purely mental process: for example a present thought may cause a memory to arise. I also explain the subsequent mind door process, which follows the mind door[5]. With regard to this mind door process I also describe the meditation processes and the attainment of the different kinds of absorption. I describe the different types of process such as the supernormal process, the reviewing process, the dying process, the fruition process, the pre-Nibbānic process and the pari-Nibbānic process[6]. These processes are only mentioned very briefly in the Manual. The dying process is closely related to the rebirth process[7]. The Abhidhamma treats them separately and explains how they are linked - after death comes rebirth. It is my hope that many people, particularly in the West, will be interested in this description of the rebirth process.

The final section of the book is concerned with the process of matter[8]. Material phenomena or qualities originate from kamma, consciousness, temperature and nutrition[9]. I explain how these material qualities come together at the time of conception, and continue through life. I also explain what happens at the death moment and afterwards. At the moment of conception the formation of these qualities occurs within 17 mind moments and then immediately new qualities begin to arise and then pass away and so ceaselessly on and on throughout life, until the death moment.

Dr Rewata Dhamma
Birmingham Buddhist Vihara
UK
25/02/2004

Namo tassa Bhagavato Arahato
Sammāsambuddhassa

CHAPTER I

CONSCIOUSNESS AND ITS FACTORS

Abhidhamma

The Abhidhamma, the special doctrine of the Buddha, is held in the highest esteem and is revered as the crown jewel of the Buddhist scriptures. All ancient schools of the Buddhist tradition had their own particular technique of Abhidhamma systematisation. However, (except for some books, i.e. the Abhidharmakosa of the Vasubandhu and the Abhidharmadīpa) most of the schools lost their Abhidhamma literature and systems, whether in the original language of Pāli or in Sanskrit. The Theravāda school fortunately preserved with extreme care the entire Abhidhamma literature, along with the associated commentaries and sub-commentaries. It needs to be understood that the Abhidhamma teachings were not discourses or discussions occurring in everyday mundane settings. Rather the Abhidhamma teachings are microscopically analysed, methodically organised, minutely defined and meticulously classified, in a necessarily highly complex vocabulary of abstract terms. Thus, owing to its immense importance, because it is conducive to one's deliverance and its excellent analytical method of treatment it is called the Abhidhamma[1], the special doctrine of the Buddha.

Ultimate Reality-Paramattha

According to the Abhidhamma, there are two kinds of realities - the conventional reality (sammuti) and the ultimate reality (paramattha). Conventional realities are the reference points of ordinary conceptual thought (paññatti) and conventional modes of expression (vohāra). They include such entities as living beings, persons, men, women, animals, trees, plants, mountains and so on.

One understands and gives names to these according to their shape, form, colour etc. However, the Abhidhamma teaching maintains that these notions do not possess ultimate validity. The objects that they signify do not exist in their own right as irreducible realities. Their mode of being is conceptual, not actual. They are products of mental construction (parikappanā), not realities existing by reason of their own nature.

Ultimate realities, however, exist by reason of their own intrinsic nature (sabhāva). These are all those of mental and material phenomena that are the final irreducible components of existence, the entities that result from right analysis of the phenomenal world. Thus, just as one extracts oil from sesame seed, so one can extract the ultimate realities from the conventional realities. The ultimate realities, therefore, are characterised not only from the ontological perspective as the true ultimate entities but also from the epistemological perspective as the ultimate object of right knowledge. For example, a so called "being", "man" or "woman" is a conceptual or conventional reality. In fact, however, the "being", "man" or "woman" is just a combination of ultimate realities. When we analyses such conceptual or conventional realities in the light of the Abhidhamma, we find that they do not possess any ultimate truth, even though this might appear to be strongly implied by the concepts. They are merely a conventional reality comprising of an assemblage of ever changing factors, of mental and physical processes. Thus, by examining the conventional realities with wisdom, we will finally come to realise that it is only the ultimate realities (paramattha dhamma) that maintain their intrinsic nature independently.

The word paramattha is a compound form of parama and attha. Parama is defined as immutable (aviparīta) or abstract (nibbattita). Attha means thing. Although the term immutable is used here, this should not be interpreted as saying that all ultimate realities are eternal or permanent. In fact, all mental and material forces are subject to change, they are impermanent and in fact are constantly changing. However, their distinctive characteristics are the same whenever they arise. Although all phenomena change, their inherent qualities do not. Take lobha (greed) for example, greed/craving arises momentarily, yet greed never loses its inherent nature, which is to cling. Thus, the best translation of the word Paramattha may in fact be "abstract" reality.

Fourfold Realities

In the Discourses (sutta) the Buddha usually analyses a being or an individual into five aggregates (pañcakkhandha), the five kinds of ultimate realities, the twelve bases (āyatana) and the eighteen kinds of elements (dhātu). In the Abhidhamma the ultimate realities are enumerated in four categories: consciousness (citta), mental states (cetasika), material qualities (rūpa) and nibbāna. Of them the first three are conditioned ultimate realities and the last reality (nibbāna) is unconditioned[2].

Although the ultimate realities (paramattha dhamma) exist within all mental and material things as the concrete essences of things, they are so subtle and profound that an ordinary person who lacks deep training in meditation cannot perceive them. Such an untrained person cannot see the ultimate realities because his mind is obscured by concepts (paññatti). The ordinary person perceives things according to their shape or form, which conventionally define their appearance. Only one who has trained deeply in meditation, and who has developed insight and right thought towards things (yoniso manasikāra), can see things beyond the concepts, realising them as the object of awareness. Thus, paramattha dhamma is described as the domain of supreme knowledge, insight.

Consciousness-Citta

The word citta comes from the Pāli root "citi", meaning "to know" or "to cognise". The Abhidhamma commentators give three meanings to the word citta. They define citta as agent, as instrument and as activity. Citta as agent is that which cognises an object, (Āramaṇaṁ cintetīti cittaṁ). As instrument citta is defined as the means by which the accompanying mental factors cognise an object

(Etena cintetīti cittaṁ). Finally, citta as activity is simply "thinking" (Cintanamattaṁ cittaṁ). A question arises: how is it that the commentators came to define citta in these three ways? The answer is that the idea of a soul or atta (ātman) is deeply rooted in the human mind. For this reason, the ancient religious thinkers have supported the idea of a soul, ātman or atta. In their opinion, it is the atta or ātman that is the thinker of thoughts, the feeler of feelings and the doer of deeds. In the view of the Abhidhamma, however, the existence of ātman is false. In the Abhidhamma it is the citta (consciousness) itself that cognises objects and all other mental states arise together with citta. Citta itself is equated with thought.

The first and second definitions prove that no ātman or "self" exists. It is citta itself that thinks. It can therefore be said that there is no thinker, only thinking.

The characteristic of citta is the knowing of an object. The function of citta is to be forerunner of the mental factors, in that it presides over them and is accompanied by them. It manifests in the meditator's mind as a continuity of processes. However, consciousness cannot arise on its own. Rather it depends on mental factors and material phenomena. Citta has a single characteristic as the cognising of an object, a characteristic that remains the same in all its diverse manifestations. What we ordinarily think of as consciousness is really a series of cittas, momentary acts of consciousness, occurring in such rapid succession that we cannot detect the discrete moments, which are of diverse types. The Abhidhamma not only distinguishes between the types of consciousness but, more importantly, it also classifies them as a unified and closely interwoven whole.

Classification of Consciousness

Classification by way of Plane

The Abhidhamma classified consciousness according to several principles. Classifications by way of planes of existence, and by nature or kind, play very important roles in the Abhidhamma. There are four planes of consciousness. Three are mundane: the sense sphere, the fine material sphere and the immaterial sphere. The fourth plane is the supra-mundane; it is also the state of consciousness. The word "sphere", which qualifies the first three planes, means in this context "that which moves about in or frequents a particular location". The locality frequented is the plane of existence. It is also called the realm (bhūmi) and is designated by the name of the sphere. However, the sense-sphere consciousnesses are experienced not only in the sense-sphere but also in the other spheres. The same is true with the fine-material sphere and immaterial sphere consciousnesses.

Thus, consciousness may be divided into four classes by the way of plane of existence:

1. Sense-sphere consciousness, which is mostly experienced in the sense sphere. The total number of sense-sphere consciousnesses is fifty-four:
   (i) 12 unwholesome cittas, (8 greed rooted, 2 hatred rooted and 2 delusion rooted)
   (ii) 18 rootless cittas, (7 unwholesome resultant, 8 wholesome resultant and 3 rootless functional)
   (iii) 24 sense-sphere beautiful cittas, (8 sense-sphere or great wholesome, 8 sense-sphere or great resultant and 8 sense-sphere or great functional)

2. Fine-material consciousness, which is mostly experienced in the fine-material sphere. The total number of the fine-material sphere consciousnesses is fifteen: 5 wholesome, 5 resultant and 5 functional.

3. Immaterial consciousness, which is mostly but not always experienced in the immaterial sphere. The number of immaterial consciousnesses is twelve: 4 wholesome, 4 resultant and 4 functional.

4. Supra-mundane consciousness, which is experienced by the noble

ones. The 8 supra-mundane consciousnesses are: 4 path cittas and 4 fruition cittas.

Thus, the total number of consciousnesses is eighty-nine: 54 sense-sphere, 15 fine-material sphere, 12 immaterial sphere and 8 supra-mundane cittas (54+15+12+8=89). Of them the first three classes are designated as mundane cittas, they are 81 in total. The final class is the supra-mundane citta, there are only 8 such cittas.

Supra-Mundane Citta and Jhāna

There are two vehicles (yāna) to obtain the supra-mundane cittas: Vipassanā yāna and samatha yāna. A person who practises bare vipassanā meditation experiences the four path cittas and the four fruition cittas. Therefore, there are only eight supra-mundane cittas for the person who realizes supra-mundane citta through vipassanā meditation. However, consider a person who first develops samatha or tranquillity meditation and achieves the first jhāna, as the foundation for his vipassanā insight. For this person the first path consciousness is also accompanied by the first jhāna, so it is known as the first jhāna stream entry path citta. Like-wise for the second, third, fourth and fifth jhāna stream entry path cittas. Thus, there are five stream entry path cittas associated with each jhānic stage. In other words, the stream entry path citta is multiplied by the five jhānas. In the same way, there are five once returning paths, five non-returning paths and five Arahantship paths. Thus, the total number of path consciousnesses is twenty. As fruition immediately follows the path citta, without any lapse in time, there are also twenty fruition cittas. There are altogether forty types of supra-mundane consciousnesses. In all there are 121 cittas: 81 mundane cittas and 40 supra-mundane cittas.

Classification by way of Nature (Jāti)

The consciousnesses may also be divided into classes according to nature (jāti). There are four such classes:

(1) 12 Unwholesome Cittas: 8 greed rooted cittas, 2 hatred rooted

cittas and 2 delusion rooted cittas (8+2+2=12)

(2) 21 Wholesome Cittas: 8 sense-sphere wholesome cittas, 5 fine-material wholesome, 4 immaterial wholesome and 4 path cittas (8+5+4+4=21)

(3) 36 Resultant Cittas: 7 rootless unwholesome resultant, 8 rootless wholesome resultant, 8 sense-sphere resultant, 5 fine material resultant, 4 immaterial resultant and 4 fruition cittas (7+8+8+5+4+4=36)

(4) 20 Functional Cittas: 3 rootless functional, 8 sense-sphere functional, 5 fine-material functional and 4 immaterial functional (3+8+5+4=20)

It can be seen that if the path and fruition cittas are multiplied by the five jhānic stages, there are 20 path cittas and 20 fruition cittas. Then the number of wholesome cittas becomes 37 and the number of resultant cittas becomes 52.

THE 89 AND 121 CITTAS AT A GLANCE[3]

MUNDANE CITTAS 81

Sense-sphere cittas 54
Unwholesome cittas 12

(1 - 8) Greed-rooted cittas	8
(9 -10) Hatred-rooted cittas	2
(11 -12) Delusion-rooted cittas	2

Rootless cittas 18

(13 - 19) Unwholesome resultant	7
(20 - 27) Wholesome resultant	8
(28 - 30) Rootless functional	3

Sense-sphere beautiful cittas 24

(31 - 38) Sense-sphere wholesome	8
(39 - 46) Sense-sphere resultant	8
(47 - 54) Sense-sphere functional	8

Fine-material-sphere cittas 15

(55 - 59) Fine-material-sphere wholesome	5
(60 - 64) Fine-material-sphere resultant	5
(65 - 69) Fine-material-sphere functional	5

Immaterial-sphere cittas 12

(70 - 73) Immaterial-sphere wholesome	4
(74 - 77) Immaterial-sphere resultant	4
(78 - 81) Immaterial-sphere functional	4

SUPRAMUNDANE CITTAS 8 or 40

Supramundane wholesome cittas 4 or 20

(82) or (82 - 86) Path of stream entry	1 or 5
(83) or (87 - 91) Path of once returning	1 or 5
(84) or (92 - 96) Path of non-returning	1 or 5
(85) or (97 - 101) Path of Arahantship	1 or 5

Supramundane resultant cittas 4 or 20

(86) or (102 - 106) Fruit of stream entry	1 or 5
(87) or (107 - 111) Fruit of once returning	1 or 5
(88) or (112 - 116) Fruit on non-returning	1 or 5
(89) or (117 - 121) Fruit of Arahantship	1 or 5

Mental Factors-Cetasikas

Along with the cittas (consciousnesses) there arise cetasikas. All mental states, mental actions, factors and mental phenomena are referred to as "cetasikas". Cetasikas always occur spontaneously, arising together with the cittas. A cetasika is defined as a mental factor that arises together with a citta and then ceases the moment the citta ceases. Without an object no citta can arise. This is also true of a mental factor, since it always shares the same sense object as that of its related citta. Whenever any citta arises at least seven mental factors also arise. This occurrence of mental factors is dependent upon the object, the individual and the particular realm that the being inhabits.

A cetasika cannot arise without citta, nor can citta arise without a cetasika; they are totally interdependent. At the moment of cognition citta and cetasika operate together. Cetasikas can be regarded as being mental properties. Citta itself is invisible; hence, one can perceive only the effect of citta, i.e. the cittasika. Citta always manifests according to the associated cetasika. For example, when anger arises it shows itself as the mental state of anger. In this case, the latter is the cetasika and the former is the citta. The arising of a particular consciousness and its related mental factor coincide. This interrelationship is best demonstrated by the following example. When clean, clear water is mixed with blue dye the only thing visible is blue coloured water. In the same way, depending upon which citta is present a state of mind or cetasika arises. However, it is citta that is chief. Its predominance can be illustrated by the following example. When it is announced, "The king is coming", the king does arrive in due course but he is not alone, he is accompanied by his retinue. Similarly, whenever consciousness or citta arises it does not do so alone; it is always accompanied by its respective cetasikas or mental factors. Citta and cetasikas always arise together, with the appropriate sense object and sense base. So, to conclude, we may say that every citta arises in conjunction with its respective cetasikas. They share the same sense object and the same base. They also cease together.

Ethically Variable Cetasikas

In the Abhidhamma there is a total of fifty-two cetasikas or mental factors. These mental factors are divided into three basic groups: the ethically variable factors (aññanamāna cetasikas), the unwholesome factors (akusala cetasikas) and the beautiful factors (sobhana cetasikas).

Of the fifty-two cetasikas, seven are classified as Universals and six are classified as Occasional. Taken together these thirteen factors are aññasamāna, that is ethically variable. The word aññasamāna literally means "common to the other". The non-beautiful cittas are called other (añña) in relation to the beautiful cittas. The beautiful cittas are called "other" in relation to the non-beautiful cittas. Thus, all thirteen factors are said to be, aññasamāna, that is common to both the beautiful and the non-beautiful cetasikas. Of them the following are called Universals or sabba-citta-sādhāraṇa (because they are associated with all cittas without exception): phassa (contact), vedanā (feeling), saññā (perception), cetanā (volition), ekaggatā (one-pointedness of mind), jāvitindriya (life-faculty) and manasikāra (attention).

However, vitakka (initial application), vicāra (sustained application), adhimokkha (decision), vīriya (effort or energy), pīti (joy) and chanda (will) are called pakiṇṇaka cetasika or Occasional mental factors. These six factors are not associated with all cittas but only with particular ones[4].

Unwholesome Cetasikas

The second group of cetasikas is called akusala cetasika, the unwholesome mental factors. They are fourteen in number and all of them are associated respectively with the unwholesome consciousnesses. Among them, moha (delusion), ahirika (shamelessness), anottappa (fearlessness of wrong doing) and uddhacca (restlessness) are associated with all twelve unwholesome (akusala) cittas. However, lobha (greed), diṭṭhi (wrong view) and māna (conceit) are associated exclusively with lobha citta, that is they have greed as their root. Dosa (hatred), issā (envy), macchariya (avarice) and kukkucca (worry) are associated only with two dosa cittas, that is they are rooted in hatred. Thina (sloth) and middha (torpor) are found in the five prompted (sasankhārika) consciousnesses. Vicikicchā (doubt), however, is associated only with the vicikicchā citta, the consciousness accompanied by doubt[5].

Beautiful Cetasikas

The third group of cetasikas is called sobhana cetasika, the beautiful mental factors, which are twenty-five in number. They are called "beautiful" because they are associated only with the beautiful consciousnesses.

Of them, nineteen cetasikas are known as "the universal beautiful factors" (sobhana-sādhāraṇa) because all of them are associated with all fifty-nine types of beautiful consciousnesses. They are: saddhā (faith), sati (mindfulness), hirī (shame), ottappa (fear of wrong doing), alobha (non-greed), adosa (non-hatred), tatramajjhattatā (neutrality of mind) and kāyapassaddhi (tranquillity of the mental body). Cittapassaddhi (tranquillity of consciousness), kāyalahutā (lightness of the mental body), cittalahutā (lightness of consciousness), kāyamudutā (malleability of the mental body), cittamudutā (malleability of consciousness), kāyakammaññatā (wieldiness of mental body), cittakammaññatā (wieldiness of consciousness), kāyapāguññatā (proficiency of mental body), cittapāguññatā (proficiency of consciousness), kāyujukatā (rectitude of mental body) and cittujukatā (rectitude of consciousness)[6].

There are three viratī or abstinences: sammāvācā (right speech), sammākammanta (right action) and sammā-ājīva (right livelihood)[7]. These three beautiful mental factors are associated with every supra-mundane type of consciousness, all together and at all times. They are, however, associated only part of the time and separately with the eight beautiful wholesome types of consciousness in the mundane sphere.

The next group of cetasikas are two in number and are called appamaññā, the illimitables: karuṇā (compassion) and muditā (sympathetic joy)[8]. These two mental factors are associated with twenty-eight types of consciousness: the twelve sublime types of consciousness excluding the fifth jhāna citta, the eight types of sense sphere beautiful wholesome consciousness and the eight types of sense sphere beautiful functional consciousness.

The last of the twenty-five cetasika is that of paññā, wisdom[9]. This mental factor is associated with forty-seven types of consciousness. Paññā, therefore, is associated with the twelve types of sense sphere beautiful consciousness, associated with knowledge and with all thirty-five sublime (mahaggata) and eight types of supra-mundane consciousness. Finally, the twenty-five kinds of beautiful mental factors are associated with the beautiful sense sphere and the sublime supra-mundane consciousnesses respectively.

THE 52 MENTAL FACTORS AT A GLANCE

ETHICALLY VARIABLES-13	BEAUTIFUL FACTORS-25
Universals-7	Beautiful Universals-19
Contact	Faith
Feeling	Mindfulness
Perception	Shame
Volition	Fear of wrong doing
One-pointedness	Non-greed
Life-faculty	Non-hatred
Attention	Neutrality of mind
	Tranquillity of mental body
Occasionals-6	Tranquillity of consciousness
Initial application	Lightness of mental body
Sustained application	Lightness of consciousness
Decision	Malleability of mental body
Energy	Malleability of consciousness
Zest	Wieldiness of mental body
Desire	Wieldiness of consciousness
UNWHOLESOME FACTORS-14	Proficiency of mental body
	Proficiency of consciousness
Unwholesome Universals-4	Rectitude of mental body
Delusion	Rectitude of consciousness
Shamelessness	
Fearlessness of wrong doing	Abstinences-3
Restlessness	Right speech
	Right action
Unwholesome Occasionals-10	Right livelihood
Greed	
Wrong view	Illimit Illimitables-2
Conceit	Compassion
Hatred	Sympathetic joy or Appreciative joy
Envy	
Avarice	Non-Delusion-1
Worry	Wisdom faculty
Sloth	
Torpor	
Doubt	

Further Classifications

Vedanā-Feeling

Vedanā (feeling) is a universal type of cetasika (mental state) and is very important in our lives. It is said, "Sabbe dhammā vedanā samodhānā", which means "all states are included in feeling." This needs to be understood in the sense that feeling is common to all experience. Whatever is experienced through our six senses, seeing, hearing and so forth is defined as feeling. Therefore, it is said, "life is nothing but feeling." Feeling can be analysed as being either threefold or fivefold. When feeling is analysed in terms of its affective quality it is threefold:

I. Sukha - Pleasant feeling.
II. Dukkha - Unpleasant feeling.
III. Adukkha-masukha - Neither-unpleasant-nor-pleasant feeling.

In this classification, sukha implies a pleasant feeling either in the mind or in the body. Dukkha implies an unpleasant feeling either in mind or in body.

When feeling is analysed in terms of its governing faculty (indriya) it is fivefold. In this classification sukha (pleasant feeling) is divided into somanassa (joy) and sukha (pleasure). On the other hand, dukkha (unpleasant feeling) is divided into domanassa (displeasure) and dukkha (pain), whereas the neither-unpleasant-nor-pleasant feeling becomes identified with upekkhā (equanimity) or a neutral feeling.

I. Sukha - pleasure
II. Dukkha - pain
III. Somanassa - joy
IV. Domanassa - displeasure
V. Upekkhā - equanimity

The aforementioned types of feeling are called "Indriya"

(faculties) because they exercise governance or control over their associated mental states, with respect to the affective mode of experiencing the object. Of the five feelings, sukha or pleasure has the characteristic of experiencing a desirable, tangible object. Sukha has the function of intensifying associated states and manifests as bodily enjoyment or pleasure. Dukkha or pain has the characteristic of experiencing an undesirable tangible object, and its function is the fading of associated states. Dukkha manifests as bodily affliction or pain. Somanassa or joy has the characteristic of experiencing a desirable object; its function is to partake of the desirable aspect of the object. Somanassa manifests as mental enjoyment. Domanassa or displeasure has the characteristic of experiencing an undesirable object; its function is to partake of the undesirable aspect of the object. Domanassa manifests as mental pain. Upekkhā or equanimity has the characteristic of being felt as a neutral feeling, its function is to neither intensify nor cause fading of the associated states. Upekkhā manifests as peacefulness.

(1) Sukha (pleasant feeling) is associated with only one citta, namely the rootless wholesome resultant body-consciousness accompanied by pleasure.
(2) Dukkha (pain) is also associated with only one citta, namely the rootless unwholesome resultant body-consciousness accompanied by pain.
(3) Somanassa (joy) is associated with 62 cittas: 12 sense-sphere cittas, 12 sublime cittas and 32 supra-mundane cittas.
(4) Domanassa (displeasure) is associated with 2 hatred rooted unwholesome cittas.
(5) Upekkhā (equanimity) is associated with 55 cittas: 32 sense-sphere cittas, 15 sublime cittas and 8 supra-mundane cittas.

Hetu-Roots[10]

According to the Abhidhamma, there are six principal hetu or roots, which condition the arising of consciousness. All states of consciousness arise dependent upon hetu, with the exception of eighteen states that are ahetu or rootless. The word hetu is synonymous with the word "paccaya", meaning "condition"; "kāraṇa" or "cause", and "mūla" or "root". In the context of the Abhidhamma, however, the word hetu specifically means root or mūla. Out of a total of six roots, three roots are identified as being kusala, that is wholesome; these are: alobha (non-greed), adosa (non-hatred) and amoha (non-delusion). The other roots, lobha (greed), dosa (hatred) and moha (delusion) are said to be akusala, that is unwholesome; they are the cause of the arising of unwholesome states of consciousness.

The Abhidhamma explains quite precisely and in great detail how consciousness arises dependent upon hetu or root. It also explains how the quality of consciousness depends on its root, whether it is wholesome or un-wholesome. There are two kinds of consciousness that are rooted in delusion only, whilst all the rest of them have either two or three roots depending upon one's state of mind.

(1) 18 Rootless cittas: these are 7 unwholesome resultants, 8 wholesome resultants and 3 rootless functionals.

(2) 71 Cittas with root: these are all the remaining cittas, which are further subdivided as follows:

- (i) 2 One rooted cittas, namely: 2 unwholesome cittas, which are delusion rooted.
- (ii) 22 Two rooted cittas, namely: 8 greed rooted unwholesome cittas (greed and delusion as roots), 2 hatred rooted unwholesome cittas (hatred and delusion as roots) and 12 beautiful sense-sphere cittas disassociate from knowledge (non-greed and non-hatred as roots).
- (iii) 47 Triple rooted cittas, namely: 12 beautiful sense-sphere cittas associate with knowledge, 27 sublime cittas and 8 supra-mundane cittas. These cittas have non-greed, non-hatred and non-delusion as roots.

Kicca-Function[11]

All states of consciousness have their own specific function. The Abhidhamma classifies all eighty-nine states of consciousness according to the following fourteen types of function:

Paṭisandhi kicca - the re-birth linking function. There are, in all, nineteen cittas that function as re-birth linking consciousnesses. At the moment of conception, of a new life, only one of these nineteen consciousnesses acts as the link between the previous life and the new life. Only one particular citta can perform this function according to the individual and the plane of existence to be inhabited. In fact, the rebirth linking citta arises only in any individual existence and does so at the very moment of conception.

Bhavanga Kicca - Function of Life Continuum.

The word bhavanga is made up of two words, "bhava" meaning existence and "anga" which means factor. Therefore, the term bhavanga means "the indispensable or necessary condition of existence". Bhavanga is also defined as being "that function of consciousness that acts to preserve an individual existence from the moment of conception until the moment of death". After the first re-birth consciousness arises and passes away, then bhavanga consciousness arises moment to moment until an active consciousness arises. In fact the three consciousnesses, i.e. re-birth, bhavanga and death, are all the same type of consciousness; it is only the way they function that is different. Bhavanga citta arises and passes away each and every moment of a being's existence whenever no active cognitive process is taking place. Bhavanga is most apparent during deep, dreamless sleep. However, it does occur momentarily and countless times during waking life in the interval between one cognitive process taking place and another. Some scholars say that bhavanga citta belongs to the unconscious mind; whereas others claim it belongs to the sub-conscious state of mind. In fact, bhavanga is consciousness itself, and therefore, one cannot say it belongs to either the unconscious or the subconscious mind. Bhavanga is actually the passive mode of consciousness, not the active mode. Bhavanga citta arises and passes away every moment during the passive phase of consciousness, it flows on and on like an endlessly flowing stream or river.

Cuti Kicca - Death Function.

This function occurs at the last moment of an individual's existence. It is the citta or consciousness which marks the exit from a particular life. This citta is the same type as the rebirth and bhavanga consciousness, which are the process-freed side of existence, the passive flow of consciousness outside an active cognitive process. It differs from them only in that it performs a different function, i.e. the function of passing away. There are nineteen cittas which perform these three functions.

The unwholesome-resultant investigating consciousness (santīraṇa) does so in the case of those beings who take rebirth into the woeful planes - the hells, the animal realm, the sphere of petas and the ghost asuras. The wholesome-resultant investigating consciousness, accompanied by equanimity, performs the functions in the case of a human rebirth where one is congenitally blind, deaf, dumb, etc., as well as among certain lower classes of gods and spirits. It functions as bhavanga and cuti in respective moments. The eight great resultants - the beautiful sense sphere resultants (kāmāvacara sobhana vipāka), with two and three roots, perform the three functions for those reborn in the fortunate sensuous realms, as gods and humans free from congenital defects. These ten cittas pertain to rebirth in the sensuous plane.

The five fine-material-sphere resultants (rūpāvacara vipāka) serve as rebirth consciousness, life-continuum and death consciousness for those reborn into the fine-material plane of existence. The four immaterial-sphere resultants (arūpāvacara vipāka) serve as rebirth consciousness, life-continuum and death consciousness for those reborn into the respective immaterial planes of existence.

Āvajjana Kicca - Function of Adverting

When an object impinges on one of the sense doors, or at the mind-door, the life continuum consciousness (bhavanga) vibrates for a single moment (bhavangacalana). This is followed by another moment called bhavangupaccheda; this is the arrest of the life continuum by which the flow of the bhavanga is cut off. Immediately after this, a citta arises turning to the object either at one of the five material sense doors or at the mind door. This function of turning to the object is termed "adverting". The five sense door adverting consciousness (pañcadvārāvajjana) performs this function when a sense object impinges on one of the five material sense doors. The mind door adverting consciousness (manodvārāvajjana) does so when an object arises at the mind door. Both these cittas are rootless functionals (ahetuka-kiriya).

Dassanādi Kicca - Function of Seeing, etc.

In a thought process occurring at the sense doors, after the moment of adverting, there arises a citta that directly cognizes the object. This citta, and the specific function it performs, is determined by the nature of the object. If the object is a visible form then eye-consciousness arises seeing it. If it is sound, ear-consciousness arises hearing it. If the object is smell, nose-consciousness arises smelling it. If it can be tasted, tongue-consciousness arises tasting it. If it is a tangible object, body-consciousness arises feeling the touch sensation. In fact, the functions of seeing, hearing, etc. do not refer as such to the cognitive acts which identify the object through sight and sound. Thus, seeing an object is not the same as knowing it. The two cittas that perform each of these five functions are the wholesome-resultant and unwholesome-resultant eye-consciousness, etc.

Sampṭicchanādi Kicca - Function of Receiving, etc.

With regard to the thought process (vīthi) arising through any of the five sense doors, there first occurs the citta that performs the function of seeing, etc. Then there arises in succession cittas that perform the function of receiving, investigating (santīraṇa) and determining (voṭṭhabbana) the object. In the case of a thought process, occurring in the mind-door only, these three functions do not occur. In this case, mind-door adverting follows immediately upon the cutting off of the bhavanga without any intermediate functions. The function of receiving is performed by two types of receiving consciousness (sampaṭicchana). The function of investigating is performed by three types of investigating counsciousness (santīraṇa). The function of determining is performed by mind-door adverting consciousness (manodvārāvajjana). All of them are rootless (ahetuka) cittas.

Javana Kicca - Function of Javana

Javana is a technical term of Abhidhamma usage that is virtually impossible to translate and is, in many ways, best left untranslated. The literal meaning of the word is "running swiftly". Here javana means running because in the course of thought-process it runs consecutively for seven thought moments or for five thought moments, taking the same object. In the case of death, or when the Buddha performed the twin miracles (yamaka-pāṭihāriya), only five javana thought moments arise. However, in the supra-mundane javana process the path-consciousness arises only for one moment. The javana stage is the function of apprehending the object and it is a very important stage from the ethical standpoint because it is at this stage that wholesome or unwholesome cittas originate. Fifty-five cittas function as javanas, i.e. twelve unwholesome (akusala) cittas, twenty-one wholesome (kusala) cittas, four supra-mundane resultant (phala) cittas and eighteen functional (kiriya) cittas; except two adverting cittas. (12+21+4+18=55)

Tadālaṃbana Kicca - Function of Registration

The word tadālaṃbana or tadārammaṇa means literally "having that object". It denotes the function of taking as object the object that had been apprehended by the javanas. This function is exercised for two thought moments. It occurs immediately after the javana phase in a sense sphere thought process, when the object is either very prominent to the senses or clear to the mind. When the object lacks special prominence or clarity, as well as in other types of thought process apart from the sense sphere process, this function is not exercised at all. After the registration moments the citta subsides into the bhavanga stream. There are eleven cittas that function as registration: the three investigating (santīraṇa) cittas of rootless and eight sense-sphere resultant (kāmāvacara vipāka) cittas.

Numbers of Functions

Of the 89 cittas, the two types of investigating cittas accompanied by equanimity perform five functions: rebirth-linking, life continuum, death, registration and investigating. The eight sense-sphere resultant cittas perform four functions: rebirth-linking, life continuum, death and registration. The nine sublime resultant (mahaggata- vipāka) cittas perform three functions: rebirth-linking, life continuum and death. The investigating citta accompanied by joy performs two functions: investigating and registration. The determining (voṭṭhabbana) citta performs two functions: determining and adverting. All the remaining cittas-javana, the triple mind element (pañcadvārāvajjana and two sampaṭicchana) and the two types of fivefold cittas perform only one function respectively.

Dvāra-Door[12]

The dvāra, or door in the Abhidhamma, means the medium through which the mind interacts with the objective world. There are six doors: eye-door, ear-door, nose-door, tongue-door, body-door and mind-door. Through these sense-doors the consciousness and its concomitants, the cetasikas, go out to meet their respective sense objects; the objects enter into the range of the citta and cetasikas. The first five doors relate to material phenomena, the sensitive elements in each of the five sense organs. Each of these serves as a door by which the cittas and cetasikas, occurring in a cognitive process, gain access to their object and by which the object becomes accessible to the cittas and cetasikas. For instance, the sensitivity element of eye is the door for the cittas belonging to the eye door process, enabling it to cognise visible forms through the eye. The same applies for the sensitivities of the other sense doors in relation to their own respective processes and objects.

Unlike the first five doors, the mind door does not relate directly to material phenomena. The mind relates to mental phenomena, that is the bhavanga consciousness. When an object is to be cognised by a mind-door process, the cittas belonging to that process gain access to the object solely through the mind door, without immediate dependence on any material sense faculty.

In total 54 sense-sphere cittas arise at the five sense doors. Of them, 46 cittas arise at the eye-door: 2 eye consciousnesses, 2 receiving, 3 investigating, 1 determining (mind-door adverting), 29 sense-sphere javanas (12 unwholesome, 8 wholesome and 9 functional) and 8 registration (11 registration cittas but 3 investigating are already counted, therefore, only 8 wholesome resultant cittas are enumerated).

In a similar way, 46 cittas arise at the ear-door, nose-door, tongue-door and body-door; with eye consciousness being replaced by ear, nose, tongue and body consciousnesses at the respective doors. Sixty seven cittas arise at the mind-door: 1 mind-door adverting, 55 javana cittas and 11 registration cittas (3 investigation and 8 wholesome resultant). (1+55+11=67)

Although 46 cittas arise at each door, they cannot arise together in one process. Rather they arise according to particular conditions, i.e. the object, the plane of existence, the individual and attention. For example, if the object is undesirable, then the eye consciousness, receiving, investigating and registration are unwholesome resultant. If the object is desirable, then they are wholesome resultants. If the object is exceptionally desirable, the investigating and registration cittas are accompanied by joy. If the object is only moderately desirable, they are accompanied by equanimity. The same principle also applies to the other sense-doors.

If one of the five sense door processes occurs in the sensuous sphere all forty-six cittas can arise. However, if the process occurs in the fine-material plane, registration consciousness cannot arise because registration occurs only in sensuous beings and in the sensuous plane. If the individual is a worldling, or a trainee, the javana cittas will be wholesome or unwholesome (according to the level of attainment in the case of trainees). If the state of mind of a worldling, or a trainee, is right attention the wholesome javanas will arise, if it is wrong attention unwholesome javanas will arise. If the individual is an Arahant the javanas will be functional.

The nineteen cittas that function as rebirth-linking, bhavanga (life-continuum) and death are known as door-free cittas. This is because their functions do not occur in the sense doors. They do not receive any new object during the present existence. However, their object is, in any given existence, generally identical with the object of the last cognitive process in the immediately preceding existence. (See details in the CMA, P132, 138)

Ālambana-Object[13]

A consciousness, along with its associated mental factors, cannot arise without an object. A consciousness only arises when an object is present. There are six kinds of object, corresponding to the six sense-doors i.e. visible form object, sound object, smell object, taste object, tangible object and mental object. Of them, the mental object has a six fold division: sensitive matter or sensitive elements of five sense doors, subtle matter (16 material phenomena, except 5 sensitive and 7 objective phenomena), consciousness, mental factors (cetasika), nibbāna and concepts (such as kasiṇa sign). Mind-objects cannot arise at the five sense-doors.

Cittas and Sense-Object according to Doors

(1) The 46 cittas that arise at the eye-door are known as the eye-door cittas, they are aware of the present visible object only.

(2) The 46 cittas that arise at the ear-door are known as the ear-door cittas, they are aware of the present sound object only.

(3) The 46 cittas that arise at the nose-door are known as the nose-door cittas, they are aware of the present odour only.

(4) The 46 cittas that arise at the tongue-door are known as the tongue-door cittas, they are aware of the present taste object only.

(5) The 46 cittas that arise at the body-door are known as the body-door cittas, they are aware of the present tangible object only.

(6) The 67 cittas that arise at the mind-door are known as the mind-door cittas, they are aware of all the six sense-objects, which may be present, past, future or independent of time according to circumstances.

Individual Cittas and Sense-Object

(1) The 2 types of eye-consciousness are aware of the present visible object only. In the same way, the 2 types of ear, nose, tongue and body consciousnesses are aware of their respective present sense-objects only, i.e. sound, odour, taste and tangible object. (10)

(2) The 3 mind-element cittas: one five-door adverting and two receiving are aware of the above five sense objects pertaining to the present. (3)

(3) The 11 registration cittas and smile-producing cittas are aware of six sensuous objects comprising 54 sense-sphere cittas, 52 cetasikas associated with them and 28 types of matter. (10+3+12=25)

(4) The 12 unwholesome cittas, the 4 sense-sphere wholesome and 4 sense-sphere functional cittas, disassociated from knowledge, are aware of six mundane sense-objects comprising 81 mundane cittas, 52 cetasikas associated with them, 28 types of matter and concepts. (12+4+4=20)

(5) The 4 sense-sphere wholesome cittas associated with knowledge,

and with the direct-knowledge that pertains to the fifth fine-material wholesome citta, are aware of all six sense-objects - except the Arahant path and fruit. These objects comprise 87 cittas (Arahant path and fruit being excepted), the 52 cetasikas associated with them, 28 material objects, concepts and Nibbāna. (5)

(6) The 4 sense-sphere functional cittas associated with knowledge, and with the direct-knowledge that pertains to the fifth fine-material functional citta (the determining citta), are aware of all the six sense-objects comprising 89 cittas, 52 cetasikas, 28 material objects, concepts and Nibbāna. (6)

(7) The 15 fine-material cittas, with the exception of two direct-knowledge, have concepts as their object. (15)

(8) The 3 consciousnesses pertaining to the base of infinite space and the 3 consciousnesses pertaining to the base of nothingness have infinite space and nothingness, respectively, as their objects. (6) (15+6=21)

(9) The 3 consciousnesses pertaining to the base of infinite consciousness and the 3 consciousnesses pertaining to the base of neither-perception-nor-non-perception have the 2 wholesome and functional types of consciousnesses pertaining to the base of infinite space and the 2 wholesome and functional types of consciousnesses pertaining to the base of nothingness, respectively, as their objects. (6)

(10) The 8 supra-mundane cittas have Nibbāna as their object. (8)

(11) The 19 cittas, which function as the re-birth, bhavanga and death cittas, have kamma, sign of kamma or sign of destiny as their object. (19)

Vatthu-Physical Base[14]

In those planes of existence where materiality applies, cittas and cetasikas arise dependent on a condition called a base. A base is physical support for the occurrence of consciousness. The first five bases coincide with the first five doors, i.e. the sensitive element of the five sense faculties. However, a base is not identical with a door, since it plays a different role in the origination of consciousness. A door is a channel through which the cittas and cetasikas of a cognitive process gain access to the object. A base is a physical support for the occurrence of cittas and cetasikas. For example, in an eye-door process many types of cittas, apart from eye-consciousness, occur with the eye-sensitivity as their door. However, eye-sensitivity is the base solely of eye-consciousness, not of the other cittas that use the eye-door. Note that the various cittas that function as re-birth, bhavanga and death citta are considered "door-freed", that is, as occurring without any door. However, in planes of existence, which include both mind and matter, no citta can occur without a base.

There are six bases, namely: the sensitive element of the eye, the sensitive element of the ear, the sensitive element of the nose, the sensitive element of the tongue, the sensitive element of the body and of the physical heart. All these bases are found in the sense-sphere. However, in the fine-material realm only three bases are found, namely: eye, ear and heart base. In the immaterial realm no bases exist at all.

Consciousness Element

In the Abhidhamma, all 89 types of citta are divided into seven consciousness elements (viññāna-dhātu):

(1) Eye-consciousness element (cakkhu-viññāna-dhātu): the two types of eye consciousness, they depend on the eye base for their arising.

(2) Ear-consciousness element (sota-viññāna-dhātu): the two types of ear consciousness, they depend on the ear-base for their arising.

(3) Nose-consciousness element (ghāṇa-viññāna-dhātu): the two types of nose consciousness, they depend on the nose-base for their arising.

(4) Tongue-consciousness element (jīvhā-viññāna-dhātu): the two types of tongue consciousness, they depend on the tongue-base for

their arising.

(5) Body-consciousness element (kāya-viññāna-dhātu): the two types of body consciousness, they depend on the body-base for their arising.

(6) Mind-element (mano-dhātu): the three types of citta that are five-door adverting and two receiving cittas, they depend on the heart-base for their arising.

(7) Mind-consciousness element (mano-viññāna-dhātu): the remaining 72 cittas, except 4 arūpa vipākas, depend on the heart-base for their arising.

Classification of Cittas according to Base

(1) The 10 sense-consciousnesses (i.e. the two pairs of five sense consciousness) always depend on the five respective sense bases, i.e. eye, ear, nose, tongue and body.

(2) The 43 cittas that always depend on heart base for their arising, i.e. 2 hatred rooted cittas, 3 mind-elements, 3 investigating cittas, 1 smile producing citta, 8 sense-sphere beautiful resulting cittas, 15 fine-material cittas and 1 stream entry path citta. (2+3+3+1+8+15+1=33+10=43)

(3) The 42 cittas that sometimes depend on a base and sometimes do not depend on a base for their arising. They are: 8 unwholesome (except 2 hatred rooted) cittas, 8 sense-sphere beautiful wholesome and 8 functional cittas, 4 immaterial wholesome and 4 functional cittas, 7 supra-mundane (except the stream entry path) and 1 mind-door adverting citta. These cittas depend on a base when they arise in the 26 material spheres. They do not depend on a base when they arise in the immaterial realm.

(4) The 4 cittas that never depend on a base for their arising. These are 4 immaterial resultant cittas, which arise only in the immaterial realm.

CHAPTER II

PROCESS OF CONSCIOUSNESS (CITTA VĪTHI)

Basic Facts

Thought Moments

The consciousness of a sentient being occurs as a process of phases in a series of discrete cognitive events, one following another in a regular and uniform order. This order is called citta-niyāma, the fixed order of consciousness. In the Abhidhamma, it is called citta-vīthi, the thought process. The word "vīthi" means a way or street but here it is used in the sense of process (parampara). A thought process consists of several thought moments but a thought moment is never called a citta-vīthi instead it is called Cittakkhaṇa (Moment of consciousness).

According to the Abhidhamma, there is ordinarily no moment when we do not experience a particular kind of consciousness. Put another way, we are always hanging on to some object - be it physical or mental. The time-span of such a consciousness is termed one thought-moment. The rapidity of the succession of such thought-moments is hardly conceivable by the mundane mind of man. It is said that within the brief duration of a flash of lightening, or in the twinkling of an eye, billions of thought-moments may arise and pass away.

Each thought-moment consists of three minor instants (khaṇa). These are uppāda (arising or genesis), ṭhiti (present development) and bhanga (cessation or dissolution). These three states correspond to birth, decay and death. The interval between birth and death is characterised as decay[1].

Immediately after the cessation stage of a thought-moment there occurs the genesis stage of the subsequent thought-moment. Thus, as each unit of consciousness perishes it conditions another subsequent one, transmitting all its potentialities to its successor. There is, therefore, a continuous flow of consciousness like a stream or river without any interruption.

The Fixed Order of Consciousness

When a material object is presented to the mind through one of the five sense doors, a thought process occurs. This thought process consists of a series of separate thought moments, one following another in a particular, uniform order. This order is known as the citta-niyāma, the fixed order of consciousness. For the complete perception of a physical object, through one of the sense doors, precisely seventeen thought moments must occur. As such, the time duration of a fundamental unit of matter is fixed at seventeen thought moments. After the expiration of that time-limit one fundamental unit of matter perishes, giving birth to another unit. The first moment is regarded as the genesis (uppāda), the last is dissolution (bhanga) and the intervening forty-nine moments[2] as decay or development (ṭhiti).

The Object

When an object enters one of the consciousnesses, through any of doors, one moment of the life-continuum elapses. (This "life continuum" is known as atīta-bhavanga) Subsequently, the corresponding thought-process runs uninterruptedly for sixteen thought-moments. The object, thus presented, is regarded as "very great" (atīta-bhavanga).

If the thought-process ceases at the expiration of javana, without giving rise to two retentive moments (tadālaṃbaṇa) and thus completing only fourteen moments, then the object is called "great" (mahanta).

Sometimes the thought-process ceases at the moment of determining (voṭṭhabbana) without giving rise to the javanas, completing only seven thought moments. In this case the object is termed "slight" (paritta).

Sometimes an object enters the sense-doors but there is merely a vibration of the life-continuum, then the object is termed "very slight" (atiparitta).

When a so-called "very great" or "great" object, perceived through one of five sense doors, is subsequently conceived by the mind-door, then the object is regarded as "clear". Similarly, when a thought process, arising through mind-door, extends up to the retention stage, then the object is regarded as "clear" (vibhūta).

When a thought-process, arising through the mind-door, ceases at the javana stage, the object is termed "obscure" (avibhūta).

For example, suppose a person looks at the radiant moon on a cloudless night. At first he gets a faint glimpse of the surrounding stars as well. He then focuses his attention on the moon but he cannot avoid the sight of stars around. The moon is regarded as a great object, while the stars are regarded as slight objects. Both moon and stars are perceived by the mind at different moments. According to Abhidhamma, it is not correct to say that the stars are perceived by the sub-consciousness and the moon by the consciousness[3].

The Life-Time of Citta

Citta (consciousness) arises and dissolves in a person at a tremendous rate of more than a thousand billion times per eye-wink and there are about 250 eye-winks in a second. So, the life-time of a citta is less than one-thousand billionth of a second.

The life-time or duration of a citta is measured by three short instants, characterising the distinct features in the arising and passing of the citta. These are: (i) uppāda- the arising instant, (ii) ṭhiti- the presence or existing instant and (iii) bhanga- the dissolving instant. These three short instants (khaṇas) are said to be "one moment of consciousness" or "one conscious moment" (cittakkhaṇa). So, the life-time of a citta is equal to the three short instants of arising, existing and dissolving of citta, i.e. it is equal to one conscious moment (cittakkhaṇa)[4].

The Life-Time of Matter-Rūpa

The life-time of matter or Rūpa is 17 times longer than that of citta. So, we can say that the life-time of rūpa is equal to 17 cittakkhaṇas, or 17 conscious moments, or 51 short instants (17X3 = 51); as there are 3 short instants in a moment of consciousness.

Thus, rūpa also arises and dissolves at a tremendous rate of more than 58 billion times per second. The difference between citta and rūpa is as follows: citta arise one after another, whereas rūpa arise by manifesting as thousands of units in a small instant and it goes on constantly arising at every small instant in time. Therefore, rūpa may accumulate to become large masses that are visible to the naked eye, whereas the fleeting stream of consciousnesses is invisible to the naked eye[5].

Six Types of Viññāna-Consciousness

Viññāna, consciousness, may be classified according to the six sense-doors and the six physical bases (vatthu), as follows:

(1) Cakkhu-viññāna - eye-consciousness
(2) Sota-viññāna - ear-consciousness
(3) Ghāṇa-viññāna - nose-consciousness
(4) Jīvhā-viññāna - tongue-consciousness
(5) Kāya-viññāna - body-consciousness
(6) Mano-viññāna - mind-consciousness

Eye-consciousness arises at the eye-door depending on the eye-base (cakkhu-vatthu). In the same way: ear-consciousness arises at the ear-door depending on the ear-base (sota-vatthu), nose-consciousness arises at the nose-door depending on the nose-base (ghāṇa-vatthu), tongue-consciousness arises at the tongue-door depending on the tongue-base (jīhvā-vatthu), body-consciousness arises at the body-door depending on the body-base (kāya-vatthu) and mind-consciousness arises at the mind-door depending on the heart-base (hadaya-vatthu).

The first five viññānas are comprised of two sense impressions each; whereas mano-viññāna (mind-consciousness) is comprised of seventy-nine types of consciousness.

Six Types of Process-Vīthi

Vīthi, or the cognitive series of consciousness, is also divided into six classes. These may be named according to either the six sense-doors or the six types of viññāna (consciousness) as follows:

1. Cakkhu-dvāra-vīthi or cakkhu-viññāna-vīthi. This is the cognitive process of consciousness connected with the eye-door or with eye-consciousness.
2. Sota-dvāra-vīthi or sota-viññāna-vīthi. This is the cognitive process of consciousness connected with the ear-door or with ear-consciousness.
3. Ghāṇa-dvāra-vīthi or ghāṇa-viññāna-vīthi. This is the cognitive process of consciousness connected with the nose-door or with nose-consciousness.
4. Jīvhā-dvāra-vīthi or jīvhā-viññāna-vīthi. This is the cognitive process of consciousness connected with the tongue-door or with tongue-consciousness.
5. Kāya-dvāra-vīthi or kāya-viññāna-vīthi. This is the cognitive process of consciousness connected with the body-door or with body-consciousness.
6. Mano-dvāra-vīthi or mano-viññāna-vīthi. This is the cognitive process of consciousness connected with the mind-door or with mind-consciousness.

The Causes for the Arising of the Processes

There are four conditions for the arising of each process (vīthi). For cakkhu-dvāra-vīthi (the eye-door cognitive process) the following conditions are required: eye-door, visible-object, light and attention. For sota-dvāra-vīthi (the ear-door cognitive process): ear-door, sound, space and attention. For ghāṇa-dvāra-vīthi (the nose-door cognitive process): nose-door, smell, air element and attention. For jīvhā-dvāra-vīthi (the tongue-door cognitive process): tongue-door; taste; liquid-element, such as saliva and attention. For kāya-dvāra-vīthi (body-door cognitive process): body-door, tangible object, firm solid element and attention. For mano-dvāra-vīthi (the mind-door cognitive process): mind-door, mind-object, heart-base and attention.

(1) Five-Door Cognitive Process (Pañca-dvāra Vīthi)

There are two kinds of cognitive process: the five-door process and the mind-door process. Eye, ear, nose, tongue and body sense bases are called "five-door" and bhavanga is termed "mind-door". Each of the five door processes are divided into four classes, according to intensity of duration of the object in question, i.e. very great, great, slight and very slight. The very great object process has two types: the process ends with registration (tadālaṃbana-vāra) or the process ends with javana (javana-vāra). (In the manual of Abhidhamma, "Ācariya Anuruddha" only speaks of the process ending with registration. However, in accordance with the law of javana and registration, there should additionally be a cognitive process ending with javana[6].)

(i) The Cognitive Process with a Very Great Object Ending with Registration

Consider the example of the occurrence of the eye-door cognitive process, when a visible object of very great intensity enters the eye-door. The associated thought process arises and ends with registration as follows:

> When a visible object and eye sensitivity element arise simultaneously, at the instant of the arising of the past bhavanga, the sense object takes one conscious moment for its full development. It becomes distinct at the eye-door at the instant of the arising of the vibrating bhavanga or it enters the avenue of the eye, and the bhavanga citta vibrates for two mind moments and is arrested. Then, a five-door adverting consciousness arises and ceases adverting to that same visible object. Immediately after this, there arise and cease in due

order: eye-consciousness seeing that object, receiving consciousness receiving it, investigating consciousness investigating it and determining consciousness determining it. Following this, any one of the twenty-nine sense-sphere javana cittas runs for seven mind moments. After the javanas, two registration resultants arise accordingly. The process then ceases with the completion of seventeen mind moments at the minor instant of the dissolving of the second registration moment. Then comes the return into the bhavanga (life-continuum) stream.

Thus, seventeen mind moments have been completed. This cognitive process is called "Tadārammaṇa vāra atimahantārammana cakkhudvāra vīthi", meaning the eye-door cognitive process with very great intensity object and ending with registration.

The Process with an Object of a Very Great Intensity

SB	"PB	VB	AB	FA	EC	RC	IC	DC	JC	JC	JC	JC	JC	JC	JC	RS	RS"	SB
ooo	ooo	ooo	ooo	ooo	ooo	ooo	ooo	ooo	ooo	ooo	ooo	ooo	ooo	ooo	ooo	ooo	ooo	ooo

Note: ooo= the three minor instants of arising, existing and dissolution of one thought moment. SB= stream of bhavanga; PB= past bhavanga; VB= vibrating bhavanga; AB= arresting bhavanga; FA= five-door adverting; EC= eye consciousness; RC= receiving consciousness; IC= investigating consciousness; DC= determining consciousness; JC= javana consciousness; RS= registration.

Explanation

ooo = The three small circles represent three minor instants (i.e. arising, existing and dissolution) of one thought moment.

SB = Stream of bhavanga or life continuum: this indicates that at first there is a stream of bhavanga cittas (life continuum) present before any thought processes occur.

PB = Past bhavanga (atīta-bhavanga): the visible object arises at the arising instant of this citta.

VB = Vibrating bhavanga (bhavangacalana): at the arising instant of this citta the visible object appears or becomes distinct at the sensitivity eye element (eye-door). The very great object takes one thought moment for its full development after its arising.

AB = Arresting bhavanga (bhavangupaccheda): the bhavanga stream is cut off with the instant of dissolution of this citta.

FA = Five-door adverting (pañcadvārāvajjana): this citta is regarded as the first citta in the cognitive process of the five-door process. It adverts the consciousness stream towards the sense object.

EC = Eye consciousness (cakkhuviññāna): the eye consciousness sees the visible object. It only makes the sense impression and transmits the impression to the next citta before it dissolves.

RC = Receiving consciousness (sampaṭicchana): this receives the visible object together with the sense impression and passes them on to the next citta.

IC = Investigating consciousness (santīraṇa): this investigates the object and the impression.

DC = Determining consciousness (voṭṭhabbana): this determines whether the object is good or bad.

JC = Javana citta (impulsive consciousness): this experiences the taste[7] of the sense object. One of the twenty-nine sensual cittas then arise (usually seven times). The twenty nine sensual cittas are: the twelve unwholesome cittas, eight each of the great wholesome and great functional cittas and the functional smile-producing citta.

RS = Registration (tadārammaṇa): this is one of eleven cittas (i.e. the three investigating consciousnesses and the eight great resulting cittas of the sense-sphere). It immediately follows javana and runs for two thought moments experiencing the taste of the sense object. At the instant of the dissolving of the second registration citta, the visible object and sensitivity element of the eye dissolve together, since their life-span of seventeen thought moments is now complete.

Note: The first and last bhavanga (SB) after registration are not included in this process. This is just to point out the stream of bhavangas flowing before and after any active thought process. Though the past bhavanga (PB), vibrating bhavanga (VB) and arrest bhavanga (AB) are also not in the process, they are process free cittas. Nevertheless, since the visible object arises and remains till its dissolution, it should be seventeen thought moments, this being the life span of a material element, so it is counted from the past bhavanga. In fact, the real thought process comprises of the five-door adverting citta through to the registration citta.

It should be noted that the entire thought process occurs without any governing self or subject behind it as an enduring "inner controller" or "someone" experiencing the thoughts. Thus, in the Abhidhamma, there is no "knower" outside the scope of the process itself. This differs from Hindu philosophy which speaks of "ātman" or atta. The Abhidhamma teaches that the momentary cittas themselves exercise all the functions necessary for cognition and the unity of the cognitive act is derived from their coordination through the laws of conditional connectedness. Within the cognitive process each citta comes into being in accordance with the cosmic law of consciousness (citta-niyāma). Thus, each citta arises depending on a variety of conditions, including the preceding citta, the object, a door and a physical base. Having arisen it performs its own unique function within the process and then it dissolves, becoming a condition for the next citta.

The Simile of a Mango-Fruit

The occurrence of a thought process in a sense door with a very great object may be compared to the simile of a mango-fruit. A weary traveller with his head covered went to sleep beneath a fruiting mango tree. A ripe mango, which had become loosened from the stalk, fell to the ground grazing his ear. Awakened by the sound he opened his eyes and looked. Then, he stretched out his hand, took the fruit, squeezed it and smelt it. Having done so, he ate the mango, swallowed it whilst appreciating its taste and then went back to sleep[8].

The time during which the man slept at the foot of the mango tree is analogous to the quiet flow of the bhavanga stream. The instant at which the ripe mango fell from its stalk and grazed his ear is like the instant of the object striking one of the sense doors. When the man awoke, due to hearing the sound, this is like the five-door adverting consciousness turning towards the object. The time of the man's opening of his eyes and looking is like eye-consciousness accomplishing its function of seeing. The time of stretching out his hand and taking the mango-fruit is like that of the receiving consciousness receiving the object. The time of squeezing the fruit is like that of the investigating consciousness investigating the object. The time of smelling the mango is like that of the determining consciousness determining the object. The time of eating the mango-fruit is like that of the javana experiencing the flavour of the object. The swallowing of the fruit, while appreciating its taste, is like the registration consciousness taking the same object as the javana phase. Finally, the man's going back to sleep is like the subsidence back into the bhavanga stream.

In a similar way, other thought processes occur when their respective sense objects enter into the avenue of the respective sense doors, such as: sound, smell, taste and tangible objects enter their respective sense doors of ear, nose, tongue and body.

Five-Door Cognitive Processes

The Cognitive Process of Eye-Door

SB	"PB	VB	AB	FA	EC	RC	IC	DC	JC	JC	JC	JC	JC	JC	JC	RS	RS"	SB
ooo	ooo	ooo	ooo	ooo	ooo	ooo	ooo	ooo	ooo	ooo	ooo	ooo	ooo	ooo	ooo	ooo	ooo	ooo

The Cognitive Process of Ear-Door

SB	"PB	VB	AB	FA	HC	RC	IC	DC	JC	JC	JC	JC	JC	JC	JC	RS	RS"	SB
ooo	ooo	ooo	ooo	ooo	ooo	ooo	ooo	ooo	ooo	ooo	ooo	ooo	ooo	ooo	ooo	ooo	ooo	ooo

The Cognitive Process of Nose-Door

SB	“PB	VB	AB	FA	SC	RC	IC	DC	JC	JC	JC	JC	JC	JC	JC	RS	RS”	SB
000	000	000	000	000	000	000	000	000	000	000	000	000	000	000	000	000	000	000

The Cognitive Process of Tongue-Door

SB	“PB	VB	AB	FA	TC	RC	IC	DC	JC	JC	JC	JC	JC	JC	JC	RS	RS”	SB
000	000	000	000	000	000	000	000	000	000	000	000	000	000	000	000	000	000	000

The Cognitive Process of Body-Door

SB	“PB	VB	AB	FA	BD	RC	IC	DC	JC	JC	JC	JC	JC	JC	JC	RS	RS”	SB
000	000	000	000	000	000	000	000	000	000	000	000	000	000	000	000	000	000	000

EC= eye consciousness, HC= hearing consciousness, SC= smelling consciousness, TC= tasting consciousness, BD= body (touching) consciousness.

The Cognitive Process with a Very Great Object Ending with Javana

The cognitive processes that end either with registration or with javana are similar processes. The difference between these two cognitive processes is that the first involves registration, whereas the second has no registration but only javana. The first kind of process arises in sensual beings in the sense-sphere. The second kind of process occurs not only in sense-sphere beings[9] but also in those beings in the fine-material sphere. It is said: “Registration occurs, in connection with clear and very great objects when there are certain sense-sphere javanas, beings, and objects present”[10].

Sense Objects

Sense objects are distinguished into three classes: the undesirable (aniṭṭha), the moderately desirable (iṭṭha or iṭṭhamajjhatta) and the extremely desirable (ati-iṭṭha). While a “desirable” object is thus subdivided into two types, all undesirable objects are simply called “undesirable”.

Whether on a given occasion one experiences an undesirable, a moderately desirable or an extremely desirable object is governed by one's past kamma. Thus, the object experienced provides the opportunity for kamma to ripen in the form of the resultant states of consciousness. The resultant cittas accord with the nature of the object spontaneously, without any need for deliberation, just as a facial reflection in a mirror accords with the features of the face.

The Procedure of Javana and Registration

Because pleasant feelings and painful feelings are diametrically opposite, cittas accompanied by the one cannot arise in immediate succession to cittas accompanied by the other. However, cittas accompanied by either of these opposed feelings can be immediately preceded or followed by cittas accompanied by neutral feelings. Thus, when the javanas are accompanied by displeasure (domanassa), i.e. as citta rooted in hatred, if there is occasion for registration cittas they must be accompanied by equanimity. If there is no scope for registration cittas, javana accompanied by displeasure will be followed immediately by the bhavanga only if the latter is accompanied by neutral feelings.

The Transitional Bhavanga

Consider someone whose bhavanga is one of the four great resultants accompanied by joy. If there are no registration cittas following a javana process accompanied by displeasure, then the final javana citta in the cognitive process cannot be followed by an immediate return into bhavanga, owing to the law that cittas with opposite feelings cannot arise in immediate succession. In such a case, the ancient teachers of the Abhidhamma hold that an investigating (santīraṇa) citta accompanied by equanimity occurs for a single mind-moment, serving as a buffer between the displeasure (i.e. the painful mental feeling) of the javana and the joy (i.e. pleasant mental feeling) of the bhavanga.

On such an occasion this citta does not perform the function of investigating, rather it takes an object different from that of the cognitive process. This object would be some unrelated sense-sphere object with which one is already familiar. The citta thus functions simply to pave the way back to the normal flow of the root bhavanga. This special citta is termed āgantuka-bhavanga, "the Transitional life-continuum". The term "āgantuka" literally means "a visitor" and some scholars translated it as "the adventitious life-continuum"[11].

The Cognitive Process without Transitional Bhavanga

This process has two types: the process is either with or without transitional (āgantuka) bhavanga. Āgantuka bhavanga literally means "visitor bhavanga", although as mentioned above some prefer to call it adventitious bhavanga. It should be noted that in a particular life, the rebirth consciousness (paṭisandhi citta), the bhavanga consciousness (life-continuum citta) and the death consciousness (cuti citta) must be of the same type. If the object is extremely desirable, investigation and registration must be accompanied by joy. A counter example would be: consider a heretic[12] whose rebirth consciousness is accompanied by equanimity while seeing the extremely desirable very great object of the Buddha and his teachings. If his javana is accompanied by displeasure, then the registration accompanied by joy cannot arise but two moments of bhavanga citta accompanied by equanimity will arise, the same type as the rebirth consciousness.

The cognitive process without transitional bhavanga and with a very great object runs as follows:

> When a visible object and the eye sensitivity element arise simultaneously, at the instant of the arising of the past bhavanga, the sense object takes one conscious moment for its full development and it becomes distinct at the eye-door at the instant of arising of the vibrating bhavanga or it enters the avenue of the eye, then the bhavanga citta vibrates for two thought moments and is arrested. Then, a five-door adverting consciousness arises and ceases adverting to that same visible

object. Immediately after there arise and cease in due order: eye-consciousness seeing that object, receiving consciousness receiving it, investigating consciousness investigating it and determining consciousness determining it. Following this, any one of the twenty-nine sense-sphere javana cittas runs for seven thought moments. After the javanas, then two bhavanga cittas arise accordingly and the process ceases with the completion of seventeen thought moments at the minor instant of the dissolving of the second bhavanga moment. Then comes the subsidence into the bhavanga (life-continuum) stream[13].

Cognitive Process of Eye-Door without Transitional Bhavanga

SB	"PB	VB	AB	FA	EC	RC	IC	DC	JC	JC	JC	JC	JC	JC	JC	BC	BC"	SB
ooo	ooo	ooo	ooo	ooo	ooo	ooo	ooo	ooo	ooo	ooo	ooo	ooo	ooo	ooo	ooo	ooo	ooo	ooo

Note: ooo= the three minor instants of arising, existing and dissolution of one thought moment. SB= stream of bhavanga; PB= past bhavanga; VB= vibrating bhavanga; AB= arrest bhavana; FA= five-door adverting; EC= eye consciousness; RC= receiving cons; IC= investigating cons; DC= determining consciousness; JC= javana consciousness; BC= bhavanga consciousness; RS= registration.

The Cognitive Process with Transitional Bhavanga

Consider a heretic whose rebirth consciousness is accompanied by joy, while seeing the extremely desirable object of the Buddha and his teachings. The cognitive process with a very great and extremely desirable object then runs as follows:

When a visible object and the eye sensitivity element arise simultaneously at the instant of the arising of the past bhavanga, the sense object takes one conscious moment for its full development and it becomes distinct at the eye-door at the instant of arising of the vibrating bhavanga or it enters the avenue of the eye, then the bhavanga citta vibrates for two thought moments and is arrested. Then, a five-door adverting consciousness arises and ceases adverting to that same visible object. Immediately after there arise and cease in due order: eye-consciousness seeing that object, receiving consciousness receiving it, investigating consciousness investigating it and determining consciousness determining it. Following this, one of the twenty-nine sense-sphere javana cittas, accompanied by displeasure, runs for seven thought moments. After the javanas, the transitional bhavanga arises, then bhavanga cittas arise accordingly and it ceases with the completion of seventeen thought moments at the minor instant of the dissolving of the last bhavanga moment. Then comes the subsidence into the bhavanga (life-continuum) stream[14].

Cognitive Process of Eye-Door with Transitional Bhavanga

SB	"PB	VB	AB	FA	EC	RC	IC	DC	JC	JC	JC	JC	JC	JC	JC	TB	BC"	SB
000	000	000	000	000	000	000	000	000	000	000	000	000	000	000	000	000	000	000

TB= Transitional (āgantuka) bhavanga, BC= Bhavanga consciousness

In the same way other thought processes occur when their respective sense objects enter into the avenue of their respective sense doors, such as when sound, smell, taste and tangible objects enter the respective sense doors of ear, nose, tongue and body.

Sense Impression or Awareness

In the five sense-door cognitive process, the meaning and the function of participating units of consciousness have been explained in detail above, giving as an example the simile of the mango-fruit. However, the five sense-door cognitive process is just an awareness of an object but not full knowledge. Thus, it is processed only to the extent to which it can be classified roughly as being either good or bad. The form, the shape, the detailed features and the name of the object are not known yet. In fact, the end of each sense-door cognitive process is subsidence into the bhavanga stream for two or three mind moments. In order to know the object, they must be quickly followed by at least two further mind moments, depending on the object. Subsequent mind-door (tadanuvattika-manodvāra) processes accordingly take the same sense object of the five-door process as a past object. The details will be explained in the mind-door cognitive process.

(ii) The Cognitive Process with a Great Object

The First Cognitive Process

There are two types of cognitive processes with the fairly great object: the first process includes the previous two bhavanga consciousness, whereas the second process includes three previous bhavanga consciousnesses. Both processes terminate with javana and both have two types, i.e. with and without the transitional bhavanga. The occurrence of the first process with the great object and without the transitional bhavanga at the eye-door runs as follows:

> When a visible object and eye sensitivity element arise simultaneously, at the instant of the arising of the first past bhavanga, the sense object takes two conscious moments for its full development and it becomes distinct at the eye-door at the instant of arising of the vibrating bhavanga or enters the avenue of the eye, then the bhavanga citta vibrates for two thought moments and is arrested. Then, a five-door adverting consciousness arises and ceases adverting to that same visible object. Immediately after there arise and cease in due order: eye-consciousness seeing that object, receiving consciousness receiving it, investigating consciousness investigating it and determining consciousness determining it. Following this, one of the twenty-nine sense-sphere javana cittas runs for seven thought moments. Then, one bhavanga citta arises and it ceases with the completion of seventeen thought moments at the minor instant of the dissolving of the bhavanga moment. Then comes the subsidence into the bhavanga (life-continuum) stream[15].

First Cognitive Process with the Great Object at Eye-Door without Transitional Bhavanga

SB	“PB	PB	VB	AB	FA	EC	RC	IC	DC	JC	JC	JC	JC	JC	JC	JC	BC”	SB
ooo	ooo	ooo	ooo	ooo	ooo	ooo	ooo	ooo	ooo	ooo	ooo	ooo	ooo	ooo	ooo	ooo	ooo	ooo

Note: ooo= the three minor instantsof arising, existing and dissolution of one thought moment. SB= stream of bhavanga; PB= past bhavanga; VB= vibrating bhavanga; AB= arrest bhavanga; FA= five-door adverting; EC= eye consciousness; JC= javana consciousness; BC= bhavanga consciousness; RS= registration.

The Cognitive Process with Transitional Bhavanga

Consider a heretic whose rebirth consciousness is accompanied by joy, while seeing the extremely desirable object of the Buddha and his teachings. The cognitive process with very great and extremely desirable object then runs as follows:

> When a visible object and eye sensitivity element arise, simultaneously at the instant of the arising of the first past bhavanga, the sense object takes three conscious moments for its full development and it becomes distinct at the eye-door at the arising instant of vibrating bhavanga or enters the avenue of the eye, then the bhavanga citta vibrates for two thought moments and is arrested. Then, a five-door adverting consciousness arises and ceases adverting to that same visible object. Immediately after there arise and cease in due order: eye-consciousness seeing that object, receiving consciousness receiving it, investigating consciousness investigating it and determining consciousness determining it. Following this, one of the twenty-nine sense-sphere javana cittas, associated with displeasure, runs for seven thought moments. After the javanas, the transitional bhavanga arises and ceases with the completion of seventeen thought moments at the minor instant of the dissolving of the transitional bhavanga moment. Then

comes the subsidence into the bhavanga (life-continuum) stream[16].

The First Cognitive Process with a Great Object at Eye-Door with Transitional Bhavanga

SB	"PB	PB	VB	AB	FA	EC	RC	IC	DC	JC	JC	JC	JC	JC	JC	JC	TB"	SB
ooo	ooo	ooo	ooo	ooo	ooo	ooo	ooo	ooo	ooo	ooo	ooo	ooo	ooo	ooo	ooo	ooo	ooo	ooo

The Second Cognitive Process at Eye-Door

SB	"PB	PB	PB	VB	AB	FA	EC	RC	IC	DC	JC	JC	JC	JC	JC	JC	JC"	SB
ooo	ooo	ooo	ooo	ooo	ooo	ooo	ooo	ooo	ooo	ooo	ooo	ooo	ooo	ooo	ooo	ooo	ooo	ooo

The Second Process with Transitional Bhavanga

SB	"PB	PB	PB	VB	AB	FA	EC	RC	IC	DC	JC	JC	JC	JC	JC	JC	JC"	TB
ooo	ooo	ooo	ooo	ooo	ooo	ooo	ooo	ooo	ooo	ooo	ooo	ooo	ooo	ooo	ooo	ooo	ooo	ooo

In the second process with the great object, the intensity of sense object is a little weaker than the intensity of the object in the first process. So after the genesis of the sense object at the eye-door three past bhavanga cittas pass by before the object becomes well developed and distinct at the eye door. At the dissolving instant of the seventh javana the object and the sensitivity eye element (eye-door) also dissolve. So, the cognitive process terminates and subsides into the bhavanga streams. Thus, this type of process is known as javanavāra, a process ending with javana.

In the same way, other thought processes occur when their respective sense objects enter into the avenue of their respective sense doors, such as when sound, smell, taste and tangible objects enter the respective sense doors of ear, nose, tongue and body.

Very Great and Great Object Process with Transitional Bhavanga

In the process with the very great object, if the object is extremely desirable the registration accompanied by joy cannot arise after the javana accompanied by displeasure. Hence, the transitional bhavanga must arise. If the object is fairly desirable, a wholesome resultant registration citta, accompanied by equanimity, will arise. If the object is undesirable, unwholesome resultant registration, accompanied by equanimity, will arise. The transitional bhavanga will not arise if the object is either fairly desirable or undesirable.

However, consider the process with the great object, the person whose rebirth consciousness is accompanied by joy. After the javana, accompanied by displeasure, the bhavanga accompanied by joy cannot arise, so that the transitional bhavanga has to arise between them whether the object is extremely desirable, fairly desirable or undesirable. Regardless of the nature of the object itself, if javana is accompanied by displeasure the transitional bhavanga must arise and then the original bhavanga accompanied by joy will arise. Thus, in the process with a very great object, if the object is extremely desirable the following sequence occurs: after the javana with displeasure transitional bhavanga arises. In the process with the great object, whether the object is extremely desirable, fairly desirable or undesirable, after the javana, accompanied by displeasure, the transitional bhavanga arises. These are the differences between the two processes.

(iii) The Cognitive Process with a Slight Object

There are six kinds of processes with the slight object depending on the number of past bhavangas. Between four and nine past bhavangas will pass initially and no javanas will arise. The determining citta will occur two or three times, after which the cognitive process will subside into the bhavanga stream. This process is also called voṭṭhabbanavāra, a course ending with determining.

First Slight Object Process:

When a visible object and eye sensitivity element arise, simultaneously at the instant of the arising of the first past bhavanga, the sense object takes four conscious moments for its full development and it becomes distinct at the eye-door at the instant of the arising of the vibrating bhavanga or it enters the avenue of the eye, then the bhavanga citta vibrates for two thought moments and is arrested. Then, a five-door adverting consciousness arises and ceases adverting to that same visible object. Immediately after there arise and cease in due order: eye-consciousness seeing that object, receiving consciousness receiving it, investigating consciousness investigating it, determining consciousness arises three times, then four bhavanga cittas arise and it ceases with the completion of seventeen thought moments at the minor instant of the dissolving of the fourth bhavanga moment. Then comes the subsidence into the bhavanga (life-continuum) stream.

Explanation

In a normal situation javana occurs seven times but if there is not enough time then it does not occur at all. In other words, since the object is not distinct and not known precisely, no javana arises to enjoy the taste of the object. Therefore, two more determining cittas arise in place of the javana to determine two more times whether the object is good or bad. After that, the conscious stream subsides into bhavanga. The sense object and the eye-door dissolve at the dissolving instant of the fourth bhavanga and bhavanga or life continuum flows on as usual after that. These processes occur in those whose sense-doors or sensitivity elements are weak; thus, even though the sense-objects are of great intensity their appearance is not distinct.

The next five successive processes should be understood in a similar way, with changes in past and normal bhavangas. For example, the past bhavanga is increased one by one as the object becomes weaker and weaker. Accordingly, the bhavanga cittas in the end have to cut off one by one as the total conscious-moments cannot exceed the life time of seventeen conscious-moments. This is because it cannot exceed the life time of a material sense-object and its associated sensitivity sense-door element. Thus, at the sixth process, the cognitive process ends after the second determining citta.

The Processes with a Slight Object at the Eye-Door

1. First Process

SB	“PB	PB	PB	PB	VB	AB	FA	EC	RC	IC	DC	DC	DC	BC	BC	BC	BC”	SB
ooo	ooo	ooo	ooo	ooo	ooo	ooo	ooo	ooo	ooo	ooo	ooo	ooo	ooo	ooo	ooo	ooo	ooo	ooo

2. Second Process

SB	“PB	PB	PB	PB	PB	VB	AB	FA	EC	RC	IC	DC	DC	DC	BC	BC	BC”	SB
ooo	ooo	ooo	ooo	ooo	ooo	ooo	ooo	ooo	ooo	ooo	ooo	ooo	ooo	ooo	ooo	ooo	ooo	ooo

3. Third Process

SB	“PB	PB	PB	PB	PB	PB	VB	AB	FA	EC	RC	IC	DC	DC	DC	BC	BC”	SB
ooo	ooo	ooo	ooo	ooo	ooo	ooo	ooo	ooo	ooo	ooo	ooo	ooo	ooo	ooo	ooo	ooo	ooo	ooo

4. Fourth Process

SB	“PB	PB	PB	PB	PB	PB	PB	VB	AB	FA	EC	RC	IC	DC	DC	DC	BC”	SB
ooo	ooo	ooo	ooo	ooo	ooo	ooo	ooo	ooo	ooo	ooo	ooo	ooo	ooo	ooo	ooo	ooo	ooo	ooo

5. Fifth Process

SB	“PB	PB	PB	PB	PB	PB	PB	PB	VB	AB	FA	EC	RC	IC	DC	DC	DC”	SB
ooo	ooo	ooo	ooo	ooo	ooo	ooo	ooo	ooo	ooo	ooo	ooo	ooo	ooo	ooo	ooo	ooo	ooo	ooo

6. Sixth Process

SB	“PB	PB	PB	PB	PB	PB	PB	PB	PB	VB	AB	FA	EC	RC	IC	DC	DC”	SB
ooo	ooo	ooo	ooo	ooo	ooo	ooo	ooo	ooo	ooo	ooo	ooo	ooo	ooo	ooo	ooo	ooo	ooo	ooo

In the same way, other thought processes occur when their respective sense objects enter into the avenue of their respective sense doors, such as when sound, smell, taste and tangible objects enter the respective sense doors of ear, nose, tongue and body.

(iv) The Cognitive Process with a Very Slight Object

In this cognitive process, there are no process cittas - only the vibration of the bhavangas. During the seventeen conscious moments of the object's life span, ten to fifteen moments will be occupied by past bhavanga cittas, two moments by vibrating bhavangas and the rest by the bhavanga subsequent to the vibration. This type of process, of which there are six, is called the futile course (moghavāra).

For example, when a visible object, of very slight intensity, arises at the eye-door the object takes ten to fifteen conscious moments for its full development. Even then, the intensity of the object is so slight that it causes the life continuum to vibrate only twice without becoming arrested. Therefore, no citta arises and the object is not known at all. After two vibrating bhavangas other bhavangas keep on running. The sense object and eye-door sensitivity elements will dissolve together at the end of seventeen conscious moments after their genesis.

The next five successive processes should be understood in a similar way with changes in past and normal bhavangas, such as; the past bhavanga is increased one by one as the object becomes weaker and weaker. Accordingly the bhavanga cittas have to cut off one by one as the total conscious-moments cannot exceed the life time of seventeen conscious-moments when a material sense-object makes contact with sensitivity sense-door elements.

The Process with a Very Slight Object at the Eye-Door

1. First Process

SB	“PB	PB	PB	PB	PB	PB	PB	PB	PB	PB	VB	VB	BC	BC	BC	BC	BC”	SB
ooo	ooo	ooo	ooo	ooo	ooo	ooo	ooo	ooo	ooo	ooo	ooo	ooo	ooo	ooo	ooo	ooo	ooo	ooo

2. Second Process

SB	“PB	PB	PB	PB	PB	PB	PB	PB	PB	PB	PB	VB	VB	BC	BC	BC	BC”	SB
ooo	ooo	ooo	ooo	ooo	ooo	ooo	ooo	ooo	ooo	ooo	ooo	ooo	ooo	ooo	ooo	ooo	ooo	ooo

3. Third Process

SB	“PB	PB	PB	PB	PB	PB	PB	PB	PB	PB	PB	PB	VB	VB	BC	BC	BC”	SB
ooo	ooo	ooo	ooo	ooo	ooo	ooo	ooo	ooo	ooo	ooo	ooo	ooo	ooo	ooo	ooo	ooo	ooo	ooo

4. Fourth Process

SB	“PB	PB	PB	PB	PB	PB	PB	PB	PB	PB	PB	PB	PB	VB	VB	BC	BC”	SB
ooo	ooo	ooo	ooo	ooo	ooo	ooo	ooo	ooo	ooo	ooo	ooo	ooo	ooo	ooo	ooo	ooo	ooo	ooo

5. Fifth Process

SB	"PB	PB	PB	PB	PB	PB	PB	PB	PB	PB	PB	PB	PB	PB	VB	VB	BC"	SB
ooo	ooo	ooo	ooo	ooo	ooo	ooo	ooo	ooo	ooo	ooo	ooo	ooo	ooo	ooo	ooo	ooo	ooo	ooo

6. Sixth Process

SB	"PB	PB	PB	PB	PB	PB	PB	PB	PB	PB	PB	PB	PB	PB	PB	VB	VB"	SB
ooo	ooo	ooo	ooo	ooo	ooo	ooo	ooo	ooo	ooo	ooo	ooo	ooo	ooo	ooo	ooo	ooo	ooo	ooo

In the same way, other thought processes occur when their respective sense objects enter into the avenue of their respective sense doors, such as when sound, smell, taste and tangible objects enter the respective sense doors of ear, nose, tongue and body.

Five-Door Cognitive Processes

In three types of process, there are four kinds of courses according to the fourfold presentation of objects:

(i) the course ending with registration (tadārammaṇa-vāra)
(ii) the course ending with javana (javana-vāra)
(iii) the course ending with determining (voṭṭhabbana-vāra)
(iv) the futile course (moghavāra)

Traditionally, according to *A Comprehensive Manual of Abhidhamma*, one type of process occurs with the very great object; two types of process occur with the great object; six types of process occur with the slight object and six types of process occur with very slight object. Altogether, therefore, there are fifteen different types of processes that occur in the eye-door. Since each of these can occur in all the five sense doors, this makes a total of seventy-five sense-door processes (15X5=75). However, in this book, the process includes the sequence that occurs without registration in the process ending with javana, see item (ii) in the list above. This type of process is further divided into two kinds: with and without transitional bhavanga. Therefore, there are three processes, the process with the very great object and two more processes, with and without transitional bhavanga. This means that there are three processes with the very great object, four with the great object, six with the slight object and six with very slight object. Thus, there are altogether nineteen kinds of processes in eye-door. Given that there are five sense doors this makes a total of ninety-five processes (19X5=95).

Cittas in Five-Door Processes

There are seven types of consciousness that participate in the five-door cognitive processes. Theses are: (i) five-door adverting, (ii) sense consciousness (one of five), (iii) receiving, (iv) investigating, (v) determining, (vi) javana and (vii) registration. The fourteen states of consciousness are obtained by taking the javana seven times and registration twice. All fifty-four sense-sphere cittas occur in the five sense doors respectively and, of them, forty-six types of consciousness arise in the eye-door: 1 five-door adverting consciousness, 2 eye-consciousnesses, 2 receiving, 3 investigating, 1 determining, 29 sense-sphere javanas and 8 registration. The same types of cittas arise in the other sense-doors with their respective objects, except that in each case the pair of sense consciousnesses will be replaced in correlation with the sense door.

Although a total of forty-six cittas arise in the eye-door, they cannot all arise together in one process. Rather they arise only as determined by conditions, i.e. the object, the plane of existence, the individual and attention. For example, if the object is undesirable, then eye-consciousness, receiving, investigating, and registration are unwholesome-resultants. If the object is desirable, then they are wholesome-resultants. If the object is exceptionally desirable, the investigating and registration consciousnesses are accompanied by joy. If the object is only moderately desirable, they are accompanied by equanimity.

If an eye-door process occurs in the sensual plane, all forty-six cittas can arise. But, if the process occurs in the fine-material plane, registration consciousness cannot arise, the function of registration being confined to the sensuous plane.

If the individual is a worldling or a trainee, the javana cittas will be wholesome or unwholesome according to their level of attainment. If the individual is an Arahanta, the javanas will be functional.

If a worldling or a trainee applies wise attention (yoniso manasikāra), wholesome javanas will arise. If unwise attention is applied, unwholesome javanas will arise.

Similarly, whether prompted or unprompted cittas arise is also governed by circumstances.

The Object and the Base

In the five-door cognitive processes, all the cittas (except for the bhavanga cittas) take their respective object in relation to the present sense-objects. For example, for the eye-door process cittas the visible form, the ear-door process the sound, the nose-door process the smell, the tongue process the taste and the body-door process the tangible object. The sense-objects are not only the object of sense-consciousnesses. The five-door adverting consciousness, the receiving, investigating, determining, the javanas and the registration cittas also occur with the same sense-object as their object. Thus, when they are occurring in the eye-door process, these cittas take only the present visible object as their object. Within that process they cannot cognise any other kind of object. One should understand this in the same way with the other sense-doors. The object of all bhavanga cittas can be any of the five-sense objects, either past or present, or it can be a mental object. This object can be one of three kinds: it can be a kamma (kamma-nimitta), a good or evil deed performed earlier during the same lifetime; it can be a sign of kamma, that is, an object or image associated with the deed that is about to determine rebirth or an instrument used to perform it; or it can be a sign of destiny (gati-nimitta), that is a symbol of the realm into which the dying person is about to be reborn.

In those planes of existence where materiality exists, cittas arise depending on a condition called a base. A base is a physical support for the occurrence of consciousness. The first five bases coincide with the five doors, namely the sensitive matter of the five sense faculties.

However, a base is not identical with a door, since it plays a different role in the origination of consciousness. A door is a channel through which cittas of the cognitive process gain access to the object whereas a base is a physical support for the occurrence of the cittas. All the five-door sense-consciousnesses are based on their respective present sense-bases, which have arisen together with the sense objects at the arising instant of the past bhavanga. The material base has the same life-span as the sense object. All the remaining cittas, including bhavanga cittas, take as a support the heart-base, which has arisen along with the preceding cittas. For example, the past bhavanga is based on the heart-base that has arisen along with the preceding bhavanga, the vibrating bhavanga is based on the heart-base that has arisen with the past bhavanga, the five-door adverting citta is based on the heart-base that has arisen along with the vibrating bhavanga citta and the receiving citta is based on the heart-base that has arisen along with sense-consciousness. The heart-base is the kamma-born material form, which occurs at every instant of the arising, developing and dissolution moments, ever since the re-linking citta arose at the time of conception. The investigating citta is based on the heart base that has arisen with the receiving citta, and so on.

The Plane

In this context, the 'plane' means the realm of existence (bhūmi), not the plane of consciousness. All ninety-five cognitive processes at the five-sense doors occur in the sense-plane. In the fine-material plane three of the sense-door processes (i.e. the nose, tongue and body) are not present, only the eye-door and ear-door process without registration and transitional bhavangas occur. Thus, a total of thirty kinds of process occur in the fine material plane. There are no five-sense door processes that can occur in the immaterial plane, since there is no base at all.

The Individuals

There are, basically, two types of individual, the worldlings and the noble ones. The worldling type is divided into four classes: the woeful plane rootless individual, the blissful plane rootless individual, the double-rooted individual and the triple-rooted individual. The noble ones also have eight classes: four path individuals and four fruition individuals. The last individual of the noble ones is the Arahant and the rest are called trainees. (For further explanation see the Analysis)

The five-door cognitive process cannot arise in path individuals because these processes last only a conscious moment. They arise in the four types of worldling and the four fruition individuals. However, non-returners and Arahants have eradicated hatred and therefore, the process with transitional bhavanga cannot arise in them.

Bhavanga

In the Abhidhamma there are nineteen bhavanga cittas[17]. If a process arises in the sense-sphere beings, it will be arising one of ten sense-sphere bhavangas. If it arises in the fine-material plane, one of five fine-material bhavanga will arise. Moreover, in the sense-sphere plane, if the individual is one of the woeful rootless, then the bhavanga is unwholesome. The resultant investigating citta is therefore accompanied by equanimity. If the individual is one of the blissful rootless, then the bhavanga is a wholesome resultant investigating citta, accompanied by equanimity. If the individual is double-rooted, then the bhavanga is one of four wholesome resultant cittas, dissociated from knowledge. If the individual is either a worldling who is triple-rooted or one of the noble ones, then the bhavanga is one of four wholesome resultant cittas associated with knowledge. If the individual is in the fine-material plane, then one of five fine-material resultant cittas will arise as bhavanga according to his jhānic states. One must understand that all bhavangas, which arise in the cognitive processes, arise in the way just described, according to the plane and individual.

Analysis of Types of Individual

There are essentially two types of individual, the worldling and the Noble ones. The worldling type is divided into four classes:

(i) The woeful plane rootless individual (duggati-ahetuka-puggala): This is a being whose rebirth consciousness is the rootless unwholesome resultant investigating citta, accompanied by equanimity.

(ii) The blissful plane rootless individual (sugati-ahetuka-puggala): This is a being whose rebirth consciousness is the rootless wholesome resultant investigating citta, accompanied by equanimity.

(iii) The double-rooted individual (duhetuka-puggala): This is a being whose rebirth consciousness is the great resultant citta dissociated with knowledge, which has double-rooted four cittas.

(iv) The triple-rooted individual (tihetuka-puggala): This is a being whose rebirth consciousness is the great resultant citta associated with knowledge, which has triple-rooted four cittas.

Those whose rebirth citta is associated with knowledge are classed as triple-rooted individuals (tihetuka-puggala). These may be worldlings or they may be Noble Ones. The Noble Ones (i.e. the trainees and Arahants) have, of course, attained this state after taking rebirth through realization of the truth, not by virtue of their rebirth consciousness.

Among worldlings, the rootless individual in the woeful planes can experience only thirty seven cittas: 12 unwholesome + 8 great wholesome + 15 rootless resultants + 2 adverting. In such beings, the functional javanas (which are in fact exclusive to Arahants) simply cannot arise nor can such beings attain absorption either by way of the jhānas or the path. For such beings, the only cittas that can arise are those that perform the role of registration, i.e. the three types of rootless-investigating consciousness.

We next consider an individual (either a rootless individual or a double-rooted individual) taking rebirth in a blissful plane. This type of individual additionally experiences the four great resultants, dissociated from knowledge, making a total of forty-one cittas. In such beings the triple-rooted great resultant cittas do not arise in the role of registration. The registration cittas only arise in rootless or double-rooted individuals.

The triple-rooted worldling individual experiences a maximum of fifty-four cittas: 12 unwholesome + 17 wholesome (minus the 4 paths) + 23 sense-sphere resultant + 2 adverting. This total number includes all nine jhānas. This total is, of course, reduced for those who lack particular jhānas.

There are eight types of individual among the Noble Ones. These are the four path types who experience path consciousness and the four fruition types who experience fruition consciousness. The four path types experience this state for just one conscious moment, while they are realizing the corresponding path insights; thereafter the paths immediately follow them. Then they become a stream-enterer, a once-returner, a non-returner or an Arahant. Of them, the individual who has gained the final fruition of arahatta phala is called an Arahant and the rest are trainees.

At the attainment of the path of stream-entry, the defilements of wrong view and doubt are eradicated. Thus, the four cittas associated with wrong view and the one accompanied by doubt are eliminated. Stream-enterers and once-returners can experience the following fifty cittas, inclusive of the jhānas: 7 unwholesome + 17 wholesome + 23 sense-sphere resultants + 2 adverting + 1 fruition. The latter will be either the fruition of stream-entry or the fruition of once-returning, according to the respective level. Non-returners, having further eliminated aversion, no longer experience the two cittas rooted in hatred. Therefore, they experience the fruition of non-returning for a maximum of forty-eight cittas[18]. We can say that, altogether a maximum of fifty-six cittas are experienced by trainees; this number comes about from grouping the three fruitions and by adding the four paths as appropriate.

Arahants have eliminated all defilements and thus, no longer experience any unwholesome cittas. The forty-four cittas they can experience are: 18 rootless + 8 great functionals + 8 great resultants + 5 fine-material functionals + 4 immaterial functionals + 1 fruition of Aranhatship. These figures are for those in the sense-sphere plane. They are reduced for those in the fine-material and immaterial planes, by subtracting the cittas that cannot arise in those planes.

CHAPTER III
MIND-DOOR COGNITIVE PROCESS
(MANODVĀRA VĪTHI)

Sense-Sphere Javana Process
(Kāma-javana Vīthi)

Sense-Sphere Javana

There are two types of process in the mind-door: the sense-sphere javana process and the absorption javana process. Of these, the sense-sphere javana process has two distinct processes: the bare mind-door process and the consequent mind-door process. The bare mind-door process in turn has two types: the process ending with registration and that ending with javana.

The Process Ending with Registration

The process ending with registration arises together with the clear object but this object has two types: (i) Present concretely produced matter or matter possessing intrinsic nature; (ii) past and future concretely produced matter, and triple time (past, present and future) sense-sphere citta and cetasika (mental factors). Of these, the process that occurs with present concretely produced matter has five different processes: with one, two, three, four or five past bhavanga process.

The first type of mind-door process, with the object of the present concretely produced matter, occurs as follows:

When one of the concretely produced objects, occurring in the present moment, arises at the avenue of the mind-door, having passed one bhavanga (mind-moment), the bhavanga vibrates for two mind moments and is arrested (the second vibrating bhavanga is called the arrest-bhavanga)[1]. Then, mind-door adverting consciousness arises and ceases, adverting to that same object, towards the mind-door process. Immediately after, one of twenty-nine sense-sphere javana cittas arises for seven mind moments and then two moments of registration resultants arise and dissolve. Then, four bhavanga cittas arise and dissolve. The object is dissolved at the instant of dissolving of the fourth bhavanga, because the life-span of seventeen mind moments has been completed, and then there is subsidence into the bhavanga stream.

In the same way, one must understand the second, third, fourth and fifth cognitive processes with two, three, four and five past bhavanga cittas having passed, with the cognitive process running until the seventeenth mind-moment is completed as shown in the table below.

Cognitive Process with Clear Object Ending at the Registration

1st Mind-Door Process

SB	"PB	VB	AB	MA	JC	JC	JC	JC	JC	JC	JC	RS	RS	BC	BC	BC	BC"	SB
ooo	ooo	ooo	ooo	ooo	ooo	ooo	ooo	ooo	ooo	ooo	ooo	ooo	ooo	ooo	ooo	ooo	ooo	ooo

2nd Mind-Door Process

SB	"PB	PB	VB	AB	MA	JC	JC	JC	JC	JC	JC	JC	RS	RS	BC	BC	BC"	SB
ooo	ooo	ooo	ooo	ooo	ooo	ooo	ooo	ooo	ooo	ooo	ooo	ooo	ooo	ooo	ooo	ooo	ooo	ooo

3rd Mind-Door Process

SB	"PB	PB	PB	VB	AB	MA	JC	JC	JC	JC	JC	JC	JC	RS	RS	BC	BC"	SB
ooo	ooo	ooo	ooo	ooo	ooo	ooo	ooo	ooo	ooo	ooo	ooo	ooo	ooo	ooo	ooo	ooo	ooo	ooo

4th Mind-Door Process

SB	"PB	PB	PB	PB	VB	AB	MA	JC	JC	JC	JC	JC	JC	JC	RS	RS	BC"	SB
ooo	ooo	ooo	ooo	ooo	ooo	ooo	ooo	ooo	ooo	ooo	ooo	ooo	ooo	ooo	ooo	ooo	ooo	ooo

5th Mind-Door Process

SB	"PB	PB	PB	PB	PB	VB	AB	MA	JC	JC	JC	JC	JC	JC	JC	RS	RS"	SB
ooo	ooo	ooo	ooo	ooo	ooo	ooo	ooo	ooo	ooo	ooo	ooo	ooo	ooo	ooo	ooo	ooo	ooo	ooo

If the object is one of past or future concretely produced matter or if a sense-sphere citta or cetasika arises at the avenue of the mind-door clearly, without past bhavanga having appeared, then two vibrating bhavangas arise and are arrested. Thereafter, the mind-door adverting consciousness arises and ceases, adverting to that same object toward the mind-door process. Immediately after, one of twenty-nine sense-sphere javana cittas arises for seven mind moments and then two moments of registration resultants arise and dissolve. After this, the process subsides into the bhavanga stream.

In this process, concretely produced matter is not the present (time) moment; therefore no past bhavangas are needed. Also, it is not necessary to count the life-span of seventeen moments. These processes are called "cognitive processes with a clear object, ending with registration".

Sixth Mind-Door Process

SB	"VB	AB	MA	JC	JC	JC	JC	JC	JC	JC	RS	RS"	SB
ooo	ooo	ooo	ooo	ooo	ooo	ooo	ooo	ooo	ooo	ooo	ooo	ooo	ooo

Note: ooo= the three minor instants of arising, existing and dissolution of one thought moment. SB= stream of bhavanga; PB= past bhavanga; VB= vibrating bhavanga; AB= arrest bhavanga; MA= mind-door adverting; JC= javana consciousness; RS= registration; BC= bhavanga consciousness.

Four Kinds of Mind Door Process

When a cognitive process occurs in one of the sense doors, two doors are actually involved: the physical sense door and the mind door, i.e. the bhavanga (from which the cognitive process emerges). What is called a mind-door process is a cognitive process that occurs exclusively through the mind door, without any admixture of the sense doors. This kind of process is called a bare mind-door process (suddha-manodvāra-vīthi).

The process that follows after the sense-door process is called the consequent mind-door process. It is like when a gong is struck once by a baton and it sends forth a continuous stream of reverberations. Likewise, when one of the five sense doors has been impinged upon once by a sense object, after the five-door process has ceased, the past sense object comes into the range of the mind door and sets off many sequences of mind-door processes. Because these cognitive processes come as the sequel to a five-door process, they are known as consequent processes (tadanuvattika manodvārika vīthi or anubandika vīthi).[2]

Explanation of Ending at the Registration

In this process, which ends with registration, the object must be only a clear object. Thus, it is said in the law of registration: "registration occurs in connection with clear and very great objects". Regarding material objects, which last for seventeen mind-moments, the teachers of Abhidhamma generally choose twenty-two material phenomena; except the two communicating phenomena and four characteristics of matter. (For more details see the chapter on matter) However, all ten non-concretely produced material objects[3], which do not possess intrinsic nature, are not true realities. Investigation consciousness and the great resultant cittas, which function as registration, take true realities as an object. True realities comprise of 18 kinds of nipphanna rūpa, untrue realities comprise of 12 kinds of anipphanna rūpa[4]. Therefore, investigation consciousness chooses only the eighteen concretely produced material objects as true objects. This is because the registration cittas take the sense-sphere objects (including the sixth process in the cognitive process ending with registration), which run with the object of past and future concretely produced matters, and past, present and future sense-sphere cittas and cetasikas.

Cognitive Process with Clear Object Ending at Javana

The Process Ending with Javana

The cognitive process, which ends with javana, has two forms: the clear object process and the obscure object process. The clear object process is in turn divided into two types: concretely produced matter and non-concrete matter. The process with the present concretely produced matter has seven different types of process: with one, two, three, four, five, six or seven past bhavangas according to the intensity of the object at the mind-door. Of these, when the present object (one of eighteen concretely produced matters of clear intensity) enters at the avenue of the mind-door, after one past bhavanga, it appears clearly in the mind-door. Then, the bhavanga vibrates twice and is arrested. Then, the mind-door adverting consciousness arises and ceases, adverting to that same object, toward the mind-door process. Immediately after, one of twenty-nine sense-sphere javana cittas runs for seven mind moments and then dissolves. Then, six bhavanga cittas arise and dissolve, to complete the life-span of the object (i.e. seventeen mind-moments). The object dissolves at the instant of the dissolving of the sixth bhavanga and then, there is subsidence into the bhavanga stream.

In the same way, one must understand other processes in which the number of past bhavangas increases and the number of final bhavangas decreases accordingly. It is a rule that the life-span of a material object is seventeen mind-moments. Therefore, each process has seventeen mind moments. If an obscure object enters at the mind-door seven different processes run in the same way as for a clear object.

1st Mind-door Process

SB	"PB	VB	AB	MA	JC	JC	JC	JC	JC	JC	JC	BC	BC	BC	BC	BC	BC"	SB
ooo	ooo	ooo	ooo	ooo	ooo	ooo	ooo	ooo	ooo	ooo	ooo	ooo	ooo	ooo	ooo	ooo	ooo	ooo

2nd Mind-door Process

SB	"PB	PB	VB	AB	MA	JC	JC	JC	JC	JC	JC	JC	BC	BC	BC	BC	BC"	SB
ooo	ooo	ooo	ooo	ooo	ooo	ooo	ooo	ooo	ooo	ooo	ooo	ooo	ooo	ooo	ooo	ooo	ooo	ooo

3rd Mind-door Process

SB	"PB	PB	PB	VB	AB	MA	JC	JC	JC	JC	JC	JC	JC	BC	BC	BC	BC"	SB
ooo	ooo	ooo	ooo	ooo	ooo	ooo	ooo	ooo	ooo	ooo	ooo	ooo	ooo	ooo	ooo	ooo	ooo	ooo

4th Mind-door Process

SB	"PB	PB	PB	PB	VB	AB	MA	JC	JC	JC	JC	JC	JC	JC	BC	BC	BC"	SB
ooo	ooo	ooo	ooo	ooo	ooo	ooo	ooo	ooo	ooo	ooo	ooo	ooo	ooo	ooo	ooo	ooo	ooo	ooo

5th Mind-door Process

SB	"PB	PB	PB	PB	PB	VB	AB	MA	JC	JC	JC	JC	JC	JC	JC	BC	BC"	SB
ooo	ooo	ooo	ooo	ooo	ooo	ooo	ooo	ooo	ooo	ooo	ooo	ooo	ooo	ooo	ooo	ooo	ooo	ooo

6th Mind-door Process

SB	"PB	PB	PB	PB	PB	PB	VB	AB	MA	JC	JC	JC	JC	JC	JC	JC	BC"	SB
ooo	ooo	ooo	ooo	ooo	ooo	ooo	ooo	ooo	ooo	ooo	ooo	ooo	ooo	ooo	ooo	ooo	ooo	ooo

7th Mind-door Process

SB	"PB	PB	PB	PB	PB	PB	PB	VB	AB	MA	JC	JC	JC	JC	JC	JC	JC"	SB
ooo	ooo	ooo	ooo	ooo	ooo	ooo	ooo	ooo	ooo	ooo	ooo	ooo	ooo	ooo	ooo	ooo	ooo	ooo

Explanation

When present concretely produced matters[5] arise, even as a clear object, registration will not arise if it is occurring in the Brahma beings realm. There are three conditions necessary for registration to arise: sense-sphere javana, sense-sphere being's realm and sense-sphere object. However, in some cases, even when the process is run with a clear object in the sense-sphere being's realm, registration does not arise. Therefore, even though the three conditions are present, registration may or may not arise. The commentary to the Vibhaṅga[6] said that, if in the cognitive process running in the dying moment the object is the present sign of destiny; and also there is a sense-sphere javana, a being and a very great object; no registration will arise. After death, the immediate rebirth consciousness and another six bhavanga cittas take that present object. Thus, there is a sense-sphere javana but the object is not a clear object and therefore, no registration will arise. The object may be clear or very great but if there is no sense-sphere being, then there will be no registration. Thus, in this process, which is ending with javana, two types of process occur, one with a clear object and the other with an obscure object.

Present concretely produced matters lasting seventeen mind

moments, to indicate their life time, include past bhavangas as well as end bhavangas. Therefore, the process of present concretely produced matters, ending with javana, constitutes seven processes with a clear object and also seven processes with an obscure object.

If an object only develops fully during several past bhavangas, then the object should be an obscure or slight object, as in the five sense-door cognitive processes. Why do both clear and obscure object processes have an equal number of past bhavangas? The reason is that, the intensity of the object does not depend on the mind-door cognitive processes but on the strength of consciousness. How many past bhavangas arise, it does not matter; if the power of mind is intensified, the process will be a clear process. Take, for example, the case of a meditator taking the present earth-element as a meditation object. At the beginning of the practice, the object appears as an obscure object, with some past bhavangas arising. However, just as his concentration develops, so to his awareness also develops and the object becomes clear. In this situation the object appears after one, two or three past bhavangas. Therefore, there is an equal number of bhavangas in both processes with clear and obscure objects.

The Cognitive Processes with Other Objects

When one of the objects, such as citta; cetasika; matter; nibbāna or a concept (except present concretely produced matters), enters clearly at the avenue of mind-door the bhavanga vibrates twice and is arrested. Then, mind-door adverting consciousness arises and ceases adverting to that same object; toward the mind-door process. Immediately after, one of twenty-nine sense-sphere javana cittas runs for seven mind moments and is dissolved. The same objects, except nibbāna, enter the mind-door as an obscure object and the same process runs as with the clear object.

SB	"VB	AB	MA	JC	JC	JC	JC	JC	JC	JC"	SB

000	000	000	000	000	000	000	000	000	000	000	000

Explanation

The other objects include the past, future and present citta and cetasika; past and future concretely produced matters and non-concretely produced matters, nibbāna and concepts. When one of these objects enters at the avenue of the mind-door, there are no past bhavangas because it is not necessary to examine them when they arise or perish. There is no distinction between clear and obscure object processes. Here, seven moments of javana is the general rule for a sense-sphere cognitive process. It is said in *A Manual of Abhidhamma*: "Among javanas, in a sense-sphere javana process, javana run only seven or six times. But in the case of a feeble process such as at the time of dying etc., they run only five times. To the Exalted One (the Buddha), at the time of the "Twin Miracle" and the like, when the procedure is rapid, only four or five occasions of reviewing consciousness occur,"[7]

The cognitive process of re-observing jhānic factors is included in the processing of the other objects. In addition, clear or obscure object processes, with and without transitional bhavanga, are also found in this process. For a detailed explanation of their object and javanas, which are associated with displeasure, see the law of registration[8].

The Cognitive Process in the Dream State

When one of the obscure objects arises in a sleeping state, it is as if we are really seeing or hearing etc. The bhavanga vibrates twice and is arrested. Then, mind-door adverting consciousness arises for two or three moments and, soon after, subsidence into the bhavanga stream occurs.

SB	"VB	AB	MA	MA	MA"	SB
000	000	000	000	000	000	000

Explanation

The Process During the Dream State

Whilst sleeping there are no cognitive processes arising, only bhavanga; life-continuum cittas arising and vanishing moment by moment. If wind or other things disturb the sleep then new objects may arise during dreaming. During the time of dreaming, one may move one's hands or feet or one may say something. These kinds of actions may happen naturally, with the communicating phenomena of bodily or vocal intimation[9]. Sense-sphere javana and super-natural knowledge or direct knowledge (abhiññā) are said to be the only causes of intimations. So, it is possible for the cognitive process, ending with registration, and javana to occur during the time of dreaming. However, there is no javana that occurs in the above process; instead only kammically indeterminate cittas can arise, which has already been explained. According to the sub-commentary of Vibhaṅga[10], two or three mind-door adverting citta arise. However, the sub-commentator, Ācariya Ānanda, himself did not appreciate this cognitive process in dreams.

Bare Mind-Door Processes

According to the above cognitive processes, there are 5 clear object processes that run with the present concretely produced matters as an object and end with registration. There is 1 clear object process that runs with past and future concretely produced matters; or past, present and future citta and cetasika as an object; and ends with registration. There are 7 clear and 7 obscure object processes that run with the present concretely produced matters as an object and end with javana. There is 1 clear object and 1 obscure object that run with something other than the above objects and 1 indeterminate (dream) process. Thus there are 23 processes in total.

Cittas, Object and Plane

There are three modes of cittas that participate in the mind-door cognitive processes: mind-door adverting, javana and registration. There are forty-one out of fifty-four sense-sphere consciousnesses.

These exclude two sets of five-fold sense consciousness (10), 1 five-door adverting, the 2 receiving consciousness (or 1 mind-door adverting, 29 sense-sphere javana and 11 registration). There are thus, a total of 41 in all[11].

In the clear object process that, ends at registration, all cittas, except bhavanga cittas, take present concretely produced matters as an object and also present, past and future sense-sphere citta, cetasika as well as past and future concretely produced matters as an object. Similarly, past and future sense-sphere cittas and cetasika take past and future concrete matters respectively as their object; Bhavanga cittas, as usual, arise with one of the objects of kamma, the sign of kamma or the sign of destiny.

In the processes that end with javana, both clear and obscure processes have the same types of object, such as: citta, cetasika, matters and concept. However, if the object is present concretely produced matter the past bhavanga run, if not, there is no past bhavanga running. A clear process can only ever have Nibbāna as its object.

The clear process that ends with registration is found in the sense-sphere only. The clear and obscure process that ends at javana can be found in thirty planes but is not found in the non-percipient plane. With regard to individuals, all processes can arise in four kinds of worldlings and the four noble ones of stream enterer, once returner, non-returner and Arahant. The dream or indeterminate cognitive process can be found in the human realm in worldlings, in the stream enterer and once returner. Non-returners, Arahanta and other beings in the higher realms have no dreams.

The Object of Mind-Door Process

Abhidhamma teachers in Myanmar have produced many different formulae describing the cognitive processes, based on the *A Manual of Abhidhamma* and other commentaries and sub-commentaries. In the case of the mind-door cognitive process they generally mention all six sense objects. These objects may be past, present, future or time-freed and can appear at the mind-door for all processes; without any differentiation. The six kinds of sense objects include: visible form, sound, smell, taste, tangible objects and mental objects. Mental objects are six fold: sensitive matter, subtle matter, citta-consciousness, cetasika-mental factors, Nibbāna and concepts. In this book, these six kinds of objects are divided as far as possible for the different processes. For example, divisions are presented such as: the present concretely produced matters; past and future concretely produced matters; past, present and future citta, cetasikas, Nibbāna and concept etc.

Ledi Sayadaw said, in Paramatthadīpanī[12], there is a fourfold presentation of objects in the mind-door process, just as there is in the five-door process. The fourfold presentation is: (i) the process of a very clear object (ati-vibhūta), (ii) the process of a clear object (vibhūta), (iii) the process of an obscure object (avibhūta) and (iv) the process of a very obscure object (ati-avibhūta). Of these, the process that ends with registration is known as a very clear object process; the process that ends with javana is known as a clear object process; the process ending with mind-door adverting is known as obscure object process. The process having a very obscure sense object only causes the bhavanga to vibrate twice without becoming arrested; so that no cittas occur and the object is not known and therefore, it is called a very obscure object process or the process deprived of cittas[13].

Most teachers of the Abhidhamma[14] made an assumption based on the following passage from *A Manual of Abhidhamma*, "when a clear object enters the avenue of mind-door etc." They said, "If the process is a clear object, there must be registration. If the object of the process is sublime, a supra-mundane citta or cetasika, Nibbāna or a concept, then there will be no registration because they are not sense-sphere phenomenon; and if there is no registration, it must be an obscure object process."

According to this assumption, no clear cognitive process will arise in Brahma beings because there is no registration. Given that the mental state of Brahma is very pure and clear, the question may be asked, why should clear cognitive processes not arise in them? In fact, the clear cognitive processes will arise in them, more than in those of beings in the sense-sphere. Also, it is difficult to understand why Nibbāna is included in the obscure object process. The sense-sphere javana cittas, which have an ability to take Nibbāna as an object, are in fact very powerful cittas in the process that reviews the attainment of the path and fruition. The realization of Nibbāna by these cittas is not obscure. However, after attainment of the path and fruition insight, one reviews and re-observes with a very powerful and clear mind. Before the process of the path and fruition, Nibbāna cannot be taken as an object. So, Nibbāna is surely the process of a clear object[15].

It is interesting to consider why the objects of sublime and supra-mundane cittas and cetasikas, Nibbāna and concepts are included in the objects of the obscure process[16]. Consider the case of reviewing the factors of jhāna after the attainment of that jhāna. Consider also, the case of reviewing the path and fruition factors after attainment of that path and fruition. When one meditates on the earth device (kasiṇa) concept, just before full development and the moment of the running of the sense-sphere javanas, these objects cannot be obscure objects, they must be very clear objects. Thus, one should understand that Nibbāna is always a clear object, while other cittas, cetasikas, matters and concepts can be either clear or obscure objects.

Consequent Mind-Door Process (Tadanuvattika-manodvāra Vīthi)

The consequent mind-door process is also fivefold: the process followed eye-door process, ear-door process, nose-door process, tongue-door process and body-door process. The process following the eye-door process is of four kinds: (i) the process taking the past object, which was perceived in the eye-door process (atītaggahaṇa vīthi); (ii) the process discerning the object as a whole (samūhaggahaṇa vīthi); (iii) the process discerning the substance (form or shape) of the object (atthaggahaṇa vīthi) and (iv) the process discerning the name of object (nāmaggahaṇa vīthi). Of these, the process taking the past object, which was perceived in the eye-door process, occurs as follows:

"At the end of the eye-door cognitive process, bhavanga cittas run as much as necessary, the object that uses the eye-door process appears at the mind-door as the past object, bhavanga vibrates twice and is arrested. Then, arises mind-door adverting citta, javana runs seven times (if the object is a clear object, registration runs twice, but if it is an obscure object, no registration arise) and then, the process subsides into the bhavanga stream."

After that, the other processes occur, as follows: the process discerning all the parts of an object as a whole, discerning the form or shape on which the visible object is based and discerning the common name of the object accordingly. The consequent mind-door processes, which follow the nose-door; tongue-door and body-door processes, run in the same order as that of the eye door. However, the process following the ear-door, runs the following slightly different sequence: discerning all the parts of the sound as a whole, naming of the sound and then, the form or shape of the sound.

Explanation on Four Kinds of Consequent Mind-Door Process

(i) The process that takes the past object is called atītaggahaṇa vīthi[17]. For example, at the end of eye-door process, bhavanga cittas interrupt for a few mind-moments and then, the consequent mind-door process follows, taking the past object of that eye-door process, which by this time has already dissolved. The object of this mind-door process can be either clear or obscure.

For example, when one sees a man with only the one process of the eye-door (and the consequent mind-door process with past object has not yet seen the man), if one sees, for instance, the head at first, one initially takes as the visible object one small part of the head. Then, by moving to the other parts of the head, the sequence of the eye-door processes and all four consequent mind-door processes run according to the size of the head. Then, taking all the parts of the visible object as a whole, the eye-door cognitive process and all four consequent mind-door-processes run.

(ii) The process is running with a past whole visible object, which is a sense-sphere object; so that, if it is the clear object, registration will arise. Here "whole visible object" is not a concept but is reality. This is because the visible object has material quality; without this it is not a whole object. This means seeing each visible object as a whole (samūhaggahaṇa vīthi).[18]

(iii) This process of a whole object runs many times, interrupted with bhavangas. Then, the consequent mind-door process runs many times, discerning the form or shape of the head, which is the base of the visible object. Here, the object of form or shape of the head is a concept. Therefore, there will be no registration, either with clear or obscure object processes, and instead the mind-door processes end with the javana (atthaggahaṇa vīthi)[19].

(iv) Then, the consequent mind-door processes run many times, taking the common name of the object as "head". The object's "name" is a concept, so there will be no registration, either for a clear or obscure object (nāmaggahaṇa vīthi)[20].

Thus, to perceive the head, the consciousness runs many processes, until the consequent mind-door process discerns the name. Then, in the same way, many more processes run, for each part of the body, such as the neck, shoulders, chest etc. After completing all the parts of the body, the whole body is taken as an object. Then, the eye-door process and consequent processes run, until the process that discerns the name of the object; finally one knows precisely that this is a man. The number of processes necessary to know the object is dependent on the size and nature of the object and whether it is clear or obscure. If one knows the common name then, after the process that discerns the form or shape of the object, the process that discerns the name of the object will follow. If the common name is not known, the process discerning the name of the object will not follow. For those who did not previously know the common name, there is no process that can discern the name of the object.

Some ancient teachers of the Abhidhamma prefer to say that, the processes that discern the form or shape of the object and the name of object are bare mind-door processes, not consequent mind-door processes. They say this because these processes do not take the past object of the five-door processes but instead they run with the form, shape or name of visible matter etc. as the object. Hence, they say, these processes cannot be called the consequent mind-door processes. Although the objects are different, they are nevertheless still a sequence of five-door processes. Therefore, all processes connected with the five-door processes are included here, in the consequent mind-door processes. Nevertheless, we cannot say that after the five-door processes, there must be consequent processes. These processes do not always run after the five-door processes. At certain times they may not always arise and instead, at the end of the process that is running with the past object of the five-door processes, there may be subsidence into bhavanga without any further processes occurring.

We now consider the consequent mind-door processes that follow the nose, tongue and body-door processes. With respect to an olfactory (smelt) object, the processes discerning the olfactory object occur one by one and take the whole smell as an object. The process discerning the base of smell takes the substance or the form of the smell as an object. The process discerning the name of an object, e.g. as a perfume, as the odour of a flower etc., takes it as its object and runs many processes, with interrupting bhavangas, until one knows fully the smell.

In the case of a gustative (tasted) object, the processes discerning all parts or types of the taste occur one by one or the whole taste is taken as the object. With the process that determines the base of the taste, the substance is taken as the object. The process discerning the name of the object runs many processes, with interrupting bhavanga cittas, until one knows fully the taste.

In the case of a tangible object, the processes discerning all parts or types of the touched object occur one by one or the whole sensation of touching is taken as the object. A process occurs that takes the base of its shape or form as the object. The process discerning the name of the object runs many processes, with interrupting bhavanga cittas, until one knows fully the tangible object.

Now, consider the consequent mind-door processes that follow the ear-door process. When one hears the word "cow", the sound of the word is taken as the present object. An ear-door cognitive process runs,bhavanga interrupts for a few moments and then the consequent mind-door cognitive process runs, taking what was heard (i.e. the word "cow") as the object. One should note that, these two processes run many times, depending on the duration of the sound that is heard. According to the Abhidhamma, within one moment, one hundred thousand Crore states of consciousnesses arise and vanish (a Crore being equal to ten million). Therefore, very many cognitive processes run taking the sound of each syllable as the present object. Their consequent mind-door processes run with the past sound of each syllable. Between these processes many interrupting bhavanga cittas also arise and pass away. After running the processes, associated with each individual syllable of the heard word, there follows another process, which takes the whole sound as an object. However, if the sound is short and of only one syllable, there will be no process occurring with the whole sound. Then, with interrupting bhavanga cittas, many processes run in order to discern the name of sound. In fact, during the processes, taking the past sound as the object, the mind does not actually "know" the sound, all that is happening is "hearing". One only knows the sound when the process runs that discerns the name of the sound. Following this process, of discerning the name of the sound, many further processes may run. These may take the meaning of the sound as the object, or the form or shape of the entity being referred to (in our example a cow).(Note that in the case of the ear-door, the process of naming runs first, followed by the process discerning the meaning, form or shape).

Saddaṁ pathama cittena, atītaṁ dutiya cetasā;
nāmaṁ tatiya cittena, atthaṁ catuttha cetasā.[21]

(The object of sound is known by the first ear-door process, the past object (sound) is known by the second mind-door process, the name of object (cow) is known by the third mind-door process and the meaning of the object is known by the fourth mind-door process.)

It should be understood however, that the process discerning the name of the sound, and the following processes discerning the meaning of the sound, may or may not run. This is dependent on the person who has heard the sound. For example, if the person has previously known the meaning of a sound, then as soon as he hears the sound he may remember the meaning. However, if he has not known it previously, there can be no remembrance of the meaning of the sound and hence, the process taking the meaning of the sound as its object may not run. If one hears a foreign language or an unknown sound, no process will run with the meaning of what has been heard. There are two conditions that support the arising of the process, which discerns the meaning of the sound: the hearing or ear-door cognitive process and recognising or having a memory of the sound.

Some teachers of the Abhidhamma suggest that three more processes run between the process discerning the name of the sound and the process discerning the meaning of the sound. Thus, one keeps the memory "this sound means such and such a thing" as a sign of the meaning according to one's previous experiences. Taking such a recognised sign as the object, a consequent mind-door process runs (sanketaggahaṇa vīthi). The mind-door process runs with the connection between the recognized sign and sound (sambandha ggahaṇa vīthi). Following this decision, the mind-door process runs taking as its object "this sound means what one has recognized as the sign, shape or form of..." (vinicchayaggahaṇa vīthi). In the same way, three mind-door processes run between the process discerning the name of the visible object and the process discerning the meaning of the object in the eye-door process.

Regarding the consequent mind-door processes, Ledi Sayadaw, in the Paramatthadīpanī, explains that it is in these consequent processes that distinct recognition of the object occurs. Such recognition does not occur in a bare five-door process itself. Take the eye-door process for example. In this, the bare eye-door process is followed first by a conformational mind-door process (tadanuvattika manodvāravīthi), which reproduces in the mind door the object just perceived in the sense-door process. Then comes a process discerning the object as whole (samudayagāhikā). Then a process occurs recognizing the colour (vaṇṇasallakkhaṇā). This is followed by a process discerning the entity (vatthugāhikā). Then a process occurs recognizing the entity (vatthusallakkhaṇā), followed by a process discerning the name (nāmagāhikā). After that a process runs recognizing the name (nāmasallakkhaṇā).

According to Ledi Sayadaw[22], the process discerning the object as a whole is a mind-door process. This mind-door process perceives as a whole the forms repeatedly perceived in individual frames by the two preceding processes (i.e. the original sense door process and the conformational mind-door process). This process exercises a synthesizing function, fusing the perception of distinct "shots" of the object into the perception of a unity, as in the case of a whirling fire-brand perceived as a circle of fire. It is only when this has occurred that recognition of the colour is possible. When the recognition of the colour occurs, one recognizes the colour, "I see blue." When the recognition of the entity occurs, one recognizes the entity or shape. When the recognition of the name occurs, one recognizes the name. Thus, Ledi Sayadaw[23] asserts that it is only when a recognitional process occurs referring to one or another specific feature that one knows, "I see this or that specific feature."

Intimation Comprehending Process (Viññattiggahaṇa Vīthi)

Intimation is that by which one communicates one's ideas, feelings and attitudes, by means of bodily movements and verbal expressions. Both have the function of displaying intention. When one sees bodily intimation, the eye-door cognitive process runs, then on comprehending the meaning of intimation, the consequent mind-door processes runs.

Take the example of showing the movement of the hand to another with the intention say of a friendly wave, or an angry clenched fist. First of all the eye-door process runs taking the visible object of the hand. Next, perceiving the past object, the consequent mind-door process runs. After this a mind-door process runs discerning the function of the hand, taking bodily intimation as its object, Finally, the mind-door process runs comprehending the meaning of the intimation, be it friendly or aggressive.

With regard to verbal expression, take, for example, hearing the sound "come". Firstly, the ear-door cognitive process runs with the present object of sound. Next, a consequent mind-door process runs with the past object of the sound. After that, another mind-door process runs discerning the intimation of the sound. Finally, the mind-door process runs comprehending the meaning of the sound as its object.

Explanation of Viññattigahāna Vīthi

In intimation, there is the comprehending cognitive process. However, this does not mention the processes that discern the whole intimation or the process, which discerns the entity or the shape or form of the object. Thus, by seeing just one small part of the hand, one cannot understand the overall intimation and meaning. There must be many eye-door processes taking all parts of the hand as the visible object. Also, there must be many consequent mind-door processes, taking the past object of each and every previous eye-door process that had discerned intimation. Then, the mind-door process runs, discerning the whole intimation. After that, the mind-door process runs again, discerning the function of the hand. Then, once again, the mind-door process runs but this time comprehending the meaning of the intimation.

In the ear-door process, if the sound is short or is just a single syllable, there is no process that runs with the whole sound. According to the number of syllables there are many ear-door processes; followed by consequent mind-door processes that run with the past sound of each ear-door process. Let us return to our example of hearing the word "come". The mind-door process runs discerning the name of "come"[24]. Then, a process runs discerning the function of the intimation of the person who has said the word "come". After that, the mind-door process runs, comprehending the meaning of the sound. These are common cognitive processes. However, some teachers of the Abhidhamma say that there are three more cognitive processes that run with a sign of the meaning, according to previous experience. Taking such a recognized sign as the object, the consequent mind-door process runs (sanketaggahaṇa vīthi). Then, the mind-door process runs with a connection between the recognized sign and the sound (sambandhaggahaṇa vīthi). This is followed by the decision mind-door process, which takes as its object "the decisive sound that one previously recognized" (vinicchayaggahaṇa vīthi).

In this section different kinds of cognitive processes have been explained in the sense-sphere javana process, as a general introduction to how cognitive processes operate. However, there are many more processes. For example, there is the process of the sense-sphere javana that runs only six moments in normal time. According to the reciters of the Middle Sayings (Majjhima-bhāṇaka) there is a process in which the registration runs for only one moment; and so on and so on. Consequently, it is not possible to explain all types of cognitive processes.

End of the Sense-Sphere Javana Process

CHAPTER IV

ABSORPTION JAVANA IN THE MIND-DOOR PROCESS (APPANĀ JAVANAVĀRA-MANODVĀRA VĪTHI)

(3) Absorption Javana (Mind-Door Process) (Appanā-javanavāra)

The process of absorption javana is five-fold: (i) jhāna process, (ii) the Path process, (iii) Attainment of Fruition process, (iv) Direct Knowledge process and (v) Attainment of Cessation process. Of these types the jhāna process is subdivided into two further types of process: the process of beginner (ādikammika) and the process of entering jhānic absorption (samāpajjana).

Take the example of a person practising kasiṇa (device) meditation. In order to attain the jhānic state, the cognitive process runs as follow: When the meditator is about to achieve a jhānic state, the kasiṇa object appears at the avenue of the mind-door, bhavanga vibrates twice and is arrested. Then, mind-door adverting arises. If the person is dull-witted, four preliminary absorption javanas occur: preparation (parikamma), access (upacāra), conformity (anuloma) and change-of-lineage (gotrabhū). If the person is keen-witted only three preliminary absorption javanas occur: access, conformity and change-of lineage. Then, (in both cases of the dull-witted and keen-witted) a single absorption javana process (jhānic citta) arises. After that there is subsidence into the bhavanga stream. Then, along with some bhavanga interruption, further processes run with introspection on each jhānic factor accordingly.

Dull-Witted Beginner's Jhānic Process

SB	"VB	AB	MA	PR	AC	CO	CL	JH"	SB
ooo	ooo	ooo	ooo	ooo	ooo	ooo	ooo	ooo	ooo

Keen-Witted Beginner's Jhānic Process

SB	"VB	AB	MA	AC	CO	CL	JH"	SB
ooo	ooo	ooo	ooo	ooo	ooo	ooo	ooo	ooo

Note: SB= Stream of bhavanga; VB= vibrating bhavanga; AB= arrested bhavanga; MA= mind-door adverting; PR= preparation; AC= access; CO= conformity; CL= change-of lineage; JH= jhānic cons.

Entry into the jhānic absorption process is as follows: Whenever the meditator wants to enter one of the jhānic absorption states that he had attained previously, the meditation object that he practices enters at the avenue of the mind-door. Bhavanga then vibrates twice and is arrested. After that there arises mind-door adverting, access, conformity, change-of-lineage and then two, three or more jhānic cittas, followed by subsidence into bhavanga. After completing the absorption state (with interrupting bhavangas) the processes recur, introspecting or reviewing the jhānic factors accordingly.

Entering Jhānic Absorption Process

SB	"VB	AB	MA	AC	CO	CL	JH	JH	JH"	SB
ooo	ooo	ooo	ooo	ooo	ooo	ooo	ooo	ooo	ooo	ooo

Explanation

In the absorption javana process, there is no distinction between clear and obscure objects. This is because the meditative attainment of absorption is only possible when the object is clearly apprehended. Likewise, there is no occurrence of registration, since registration follows only after sense-sphere javana, in sense-sphere beings and with sense-sphere objects.

In the absorption javana process then, any one of eight sense-sphere javanas, accompanied by knowledge, arises and ceases four or three times. These occur in due order as preparation, access, conformity and change-of-lineage. Immediately after they cease, any one of the twenty-six sublime or supramundane javanas arises in the process of absorption in accordance with the way the mind is conveyed. After that, at the end of absorption, there is subsidence into the bhavanga stream.

For the person who is dull-witted, since his wisdom is slow, it takes four preliminary javanas in order to achieve a jhāna state. These are: preparation, access, conformity and change-of-lineage.

It is called preparation because it prepares the mental continuum for the attainment to follow. The next is called access because it arises in proximity to the attainment. The third moment is called conformity because it arises in conformity with both the preceding moments and the subsequent absorption. The fourth moment is called change-of-lineage. In the case of jhānic attainment, it receives this name because it overcomes the sense-sphere lineage and evolves the lineage of sublime citta. In the case of the first path attainment, this moment is called change-of-lineage because it marks the transition, from the lineage of worldlings to the lineage of the noble ones. This word change-of-lineage (gotrabhū) is called "cleansing (vodāna)", for it is the moment of transition to the higher paths and fruitions. In the keen-witted person, who has quick wisdom, preparation is omitted and thus, only three preliminary sense-sphere javanas occur prior to absorption.

Attainment of Fine-Material Jhāna

It will be beneficial for the reader to comprehend the process of jhānic absorptions, if it is explained here, and how one can attain the jhānas. Jhāna is a state of absorption on an object and in fact, it is a combination of five absorption factors: (i) initial application (vitakka), which directs the mind towards the object; (ii) sustained application (vicāra), which examines the object again and again; (iii) zest or joy (pīti), which takes interest in the object; (iv) feeling (vedanā) of which there are two kinds, pleasant feeling (sukha) for the first four jhānas and neutral feeling or equanimity (upekkhā) for the fifth jhāna; (v) one-pointedness of the mind (ekaggatā) or concentration (samādhi). These jhānic factors support the mind that is to be fixed on an object. They can be developed by the practice of tranquillity (samatha) meditation. The mind is normally not calm or tranquil. It is constantly agitated by five mental hindrances, such as: sensuous desire, ill-will, sloth and torpor, restlessness and worry, and doubt. These hindrances can be overcome and temporarily removed by tranquillity meditation.

How to practice? First, one has to choose a suitable object. Let us choose earth-circle (pathavī kasiṇa) for an example, as an object of meditation. A tray of about twelve inches in diameter is filled evenly with dawn-coloured clay or earth. This object is placed at a suitable distance, so that one can look at it comfortably. One has to practise meditation concentrating on that object saying mentally "earth, earth or pathavī, pathavī" in order to develop three signs. The kasiṇa circle that one is seeing is known as the preparatory sign (parikamma-nimitta).

Now the five jhānic factors are being developed slowly; the initial application directs the mind towards the object, it temporarily dispels sloth and torpor; sustained application sustains the mind on the object, it also temporarily dispels doubt; zest develops pleasurable interest in the object, it also temporarily inhabits ill-will; pleasant feeling holds the mind to stay longer on the object by its bliss, it temporarily removes restlessness and worry; one-pointedness of the mind fixes the mind and its concomitants on the object to reach the state of concentration, it temporarily dispels sensuous desire.

When the hindrances subside temporarily, the mind does not wander away from the object as frequently as before and concentration is developed to some extent. At this stage, the meditator can see the earth circle with closed eyes, just as if seeing it with open eyes. This visualized image is called the acquired or learning sign (uggaha-nimitta)

Then, one meditates on this acquired sign with closed eyes, saying mentally "earth, earth" as before. When one develops a higher degree of concentration, the sign suddenly changes to a brighter colour and the surface of the image becomes as smooth as a mirror. This new sign or image, that is bright, is known as the counter sign (paṭibhāga-nimitta). At the time of the learning sign, the meditator sees all the defects as in the original device but at the time of counterpart sign the meditator sees no defects; as it is a very bright and smooth object. As soon as the counterpart sign arises, the concentration develops to a state of neighbourhood concentration (upacāra samādhi). At this stage the five jhānic factors become distinct and strong, zest and happiness are so predominant that the meditator experiences ecstatic joy and bliss, which he has never experienced before. The meditator now lets the counterpart sign spread endlessly, in all directions, by his will power, whilst continuing to meditate on "earth, earth" as before. Eventually he gains jhānic samādhi, absorption concentration. At this stage, he can enjoy the tranquillity, serenity, joy and bliss of jhāna again and again as much as he wishes. It is said that the meditator can remain in absorption for many hours or up to seven days. During this meditative absorption time, there is a complete suspension of the fivefold sense activities and of the fivefold hindrances. The state of consciousness is fully alert and lucid.

In the first jhānic state, all five jhānic factors are present. Then by meditating on the same counterpart sign further and eliminating the lower jhānic factors one by one a meditator can attain the higher jhānic states. He attains the second jhānic state when initial application is eliminated, the third jhānic state when sustained application is further eliminated, the fourth jhānic state when zest is eliminated and finally, the fifth jhāna when happiness is replaced by equanimity and the mind remains with pure equanimity.

Attainment of Immaterial Jhāna

The one who has developed the five fine-material jhānas would like to attain immaterial jhānas because he realizes the material body is unsatisfactory and it is subject to suffering, due to heat and cold, thirst, disease, old age and death. When he becomes disgusted with the material body, he first develops the fifth fine-material jhāna, by meditating on the counterpart sign of the object (say the earth kasiṇa). Then, he comes out of the fifth jhāna, though the counterpart sign remains in his mind he neglects it, and tries to concentrate on the space left by it, and keeps meditating on that object, the space, continuously. When his mild attachment (nikanti) for the counterpart sign disappears, unfolding infinite space, he continues concentrating on this infinite space continuously, till he reaches the first immaterial jhānic state. This jhāna is called consciousness pertaining to the base of space[1].

Then, he continues his meditation on the consciousness pertaining to the base of infinite space as consciousness. He meditates on this consciousness repeatedly, till he reaches the second immaterial jhānic state. This jhāna is known as consciousness pertaining to the base of infinite consciousness[2]. To develop the third immaterial jhāna, he gives attention to the nothingness of consciousness repeatedly, as there is nothing whatsoever (natthi kiñci), till he attains the third jhānic state. This jhāna is called consciousness pertaining to the base of nothingness[3].

By taking the consciousness of the third immaterial jhāna as the object of meditation, he can further develop the fourth immaterial jhāna. This jhāna is called consciousness pertaining to the base of neither perception nor non-perception[4]. It refers to the fact that the fourth immaterial jhāna consciousness is so subtle and refined that one cannot definitely say whether there is a consciousness or not. Consciousness is no longer perceivable at this jhānic stage.

All four immaterial jhānas belong to the category of the fifth jhāna because they are based on the fifth fine-material jhāna. They all have the same two jhānic factors: equanimity and one pointedness of mind. It should be noted that the five fine-material jhānas differ from one another in the number of jhānic factors, whereas the four immaterial jhānas differ from one another in the object of meditation.

72 Jhāna Processes

There are five fine material jhāna and four immaterial (5+4=9), multiplied by wholesome and functional jhānas, becomes eighteen processes (9X2=18), again multiply by the beginner's process and the process of one who attained, it becomes thirty-six processes (18X2=36); and multiplied by the two individuals, dull-witted and keen-witted, it becomes seventy-two process (36X2=72). In the other order, the first jhāna multiplied by the two wholesome and functional processes, multiplied by the two individuals (2X2=4), and each having two types, dull and keen witted (4X2=8), there are, therefore, eight different processes in the first jhāna, and the same in the second, third and fourth jhāna (8X4=32). The fifth jhāna is five-fold: one fine material jhāna and four immaterial, multiplied by wholesome and functional, each multiplied by two individuals and again multiplied by different types of individual (5X2=10X2=20X2=40). Thus, there are seventy-two jhāna processes (32+40=72) in total.

Reviewing Process

After attainment of a jhānic state, or emerging from an absorption state that had already been attained previously, one reviews or introspects on all jhānic factors one by one, which is called the reviewing process. These processes are the same as the sense-sphere javana and bare mind-door process. In this process, some teachers suggest five moments of javanas arise. However, the reviewing of the jhānic factors is performed by a sense-sphere process. According to the law of javana, in the normal sense-sphere, javana arise seven times. When the Buddha performed the twin miracle and the like, the procedure was rapid, so only four or five javanas arose in the reviewing process. The twin miracle was a feat of psychic power, which the Buddha performed on several occasions during his life time. By this miracle, the Buddha displays his body as emitting streams of fire and water simultaneously. He performed this miracle by entering into the fifth jhāna, separately and in quick succession, using the fire kasiṇa and the water kasiṇa, and then determining to display fire and water issuing forth from his body. After emerging from each jhāna the Buddha reviewed its factors and he did this by an extremely rapid javana process, which runs for only four or five javana cittas. In this process, the objects are sublime jhānic factors, so that there is no registration.

192 Reviewing Processes

Reviewing process runs with each of the jhānic factors. There are five jhānic factors in each of the eight types of first jhāna, so there are forty reviewing processes in the first jhāna (8X5=40). There are four factors in each of the eight second jhāna, so there are a total of thirty-two reviewing processes in the second jhāna (8X4=32). There are three factors in each of the eight third jhāna, consequently twenty-four reviewing processes in the third jhāna (8X3=24). There are two factors in each of the eight fourth jhāna and so sixteen reviewing processes in the fourth jhāna (8X2=16). Each of the forty types of fifth jhāna has two factors, so there are eighty reviewing processes in the fifth jhāna (40X2=80). Thus, one hundred and ninety-two (192) reviewing processes in total.

Consciousness and Objects in the Jhānic Process

In the beginner's first jhāna process, the following cittas participate: 1 mind-door adverting citta, 4 sense-sphere javana cittas; that is, three rooted wholesome and functional cittas accompanied by joy and associated with knowledge; 2 first jhāna wholesome and functional cittas, making seven in total. Of these, the javana cittas function as preparation, access, conformity and change-of-lineage javanas. Here, the first jhāna is accompanied by joy, so that these four javana cittas are also accompanied by joy and if these processes arise in the worldling or trainee, the jhāna cittas must be wholesome. However, if they arise in Arahant, it must be functional jhāna citta.

Mind-door adverting and all jhāna cittas, except bhavanga cittas, arise with one of twenty-five conceptual objects, these are the objects of the fine material jhānic cittas, and excluded the concept of being that is the object of the equanimous sublime state (upekkhā-brahmavihāra).

Plane, Individual and Bhavanga

Traditional Myanmar Abhidhamma teachers say that the beginner's first jhāna process arises in the seven sensuous blissful planes. They arise in four noble ones and in one worldling whose birth is triple rooted in the sense-sphere resultant citta and who has attained first jhāna. The process arises in the sensuous blissful plane; therefore, one of four sense-sphere triple rooted resultant cittas functions as the bhavanga.

The beginner's processes for the second jhāna etc. are similar to those of the first jhāna, it is only necessary to add planes and bhavangas. For example, the second jhāna process of the beginner arises in the seven sensuous blissful planes and also the first jhāna plane of the Brahma world. Further more, one of four sense-sphere triple rooted resultant cittas and the first jhāna resultant citta function as bhavanga. In the third jhāna process it is necessary to add the second jhāna plane and the second jhāna resultant citta. The one who has attained the fourth jhāna will be reborn only in the third jhāna plane, so that the fourth jhāna process arises only in the seven sensuous blissful planes, first and second jhāna plane and no further planes need to be added. One who was in the second jhāna plane, if his birth consciousness was the third jhānic resultant, in the fifth jhāna process we must add the third jhāna plane and the fourth jhāna resultant citta functions as bhavanga.

The first immaterial jhāna process arises in the sensuous blissful plane and fifteen fine material jhānic realms, except for the realm of non-percipient beings. In the second immaterial jhāna process the realm of the first immaterial jhāna is added and so, in the third immaterial jhāna process the realm of the second immaterial jhāna is added and in the fourth immaterial jhāna process the realm of the third immaterial jhāna. In the same way, one has to add bhavanga cittas accordingly.

Thus, if human or celestial beings, during their time living in the sensuous plane, practise jhānic meditation and attain the first jhāna, the beginner's first jhāna process arises in the sensuous blissful plane. When he dies and is reborn in the realm of the first fine material jhāna, the jhānic state, which he attained in the sensuous plane, remains in that Brahma being, therefore, there is no beginner's process of the first jhāna. However, if he lives in the jhānic absorption, it is only that of a previously attained jhānic process (samāpajjana vīthi). Like-wise, the process of the beginner's second jhāna is not in the second jhāna realm but in the sensuous blissful plane or the realm of the first jhāna. In fact, the beginner's jhānic process of the higher realm arises only in the lower realm.

However, Mahagandhayone Sayadaw, Ashin Janakābhivaṭsa has said the following: For one who has attained the first or second jhāna etc., in seven sensuous blissful realms, when he dies, the jhāna disappears but takes rebirth in the respective jhānic Brahma realm, as the result of jhānic wholesome kamma and the jhānic resultant citta functions as rebirth and bhavanga citta. Therefore, Brahmas, if they do not have any other object, live in the absorption state, as if living in the state of jhāna. Indeed, when they are re-born in the first jhānic Brahma world, they have to practice again to attain that jhāna. If they do not practice, there will be no previously attained first jhāna process. Also if they practise again in the first jhānic realm, then there arises the beginner's first jhāna process. In the same way, the one who has attained the second jhāna etc., in the sensuous blissful realm, or the first jhānic realm, after death is re-born in the second jhānic realm. The jhānas that he attained in the previous existence have disappeared; therefore he has to practise to achieve the first and second jhāna etc., whatever was achieved in the previous existence. Thus, the beginner's first jhāna process can arise in all seven sensuous blissful planes and fifteen fine material realms.

The Object

The objects of the beginner's second jhāna process are ten kasiṇa, etc. The objects of the second, third and fourth are ten kasiṇa; the concept of beings that is the object of loving-kindness, compassion and sympathetic joy of sublime meditation and the concept of respiration that is in-breath and out-breath, fourteen in total. The object of the fifth jhāna are ten kasiṇa, concept of being that is the object of equanimity of sublime meditation and concept of respiration, twelve in total. The objects of the four immaterial jhāna processes are infinite space, first immaterial jhāna citta, nothingness and third immaterial jhāna citta respectively.

Process of Entering Jhānic Absorption

One who has attained all nine jhānas in the sensuous plane, he can enter jhānic absorptions. In addition, one can attain all nine jhānas in the first jhānic realm. Nine jhānas can be found in the pure abodes and in the highest realm. Brahmas in the pure abodes must have experienced lower fine material jhānas and immaterial jhāna absorptions, to achieve higher knowledge or supernormal powers (abhiññā), therefore, the process of entering jhānic absorptions can be found in the seven sensuous blissful realms and the fifteen fine-material realms. Those immaterial Brahmas in the higher realms, will not get lower jhānas and will not practise to have them, thus, the process of entering the fine-material jhāna does not arise in the first immaterial realm instead only the four kinds of process of entering immaterial absorption arise. However, the first jhāna process will not arise in the second immaterial realm and arises only in the higher three jhāna processes. In the third immaterial realm two higher jhāna processes arise and in the fourth immaterial realm only the fourth jhāna process arises.

Reviewing Process

In total seventeen cittas participate in the reviewing processes, mind-door adverting citta and sixteen sense-sphere javana (wholesome and functional). If the individual is a triple rooted worldling, or a trainee, there arises one of the wholesome javanas, and if the individual is an Arahant, the javana is merely functional.

The objects of all cittas in this process, except for bhavangas, are the jhānic factors. If the reviewing process follows after the first fine-material jhāna, the object is one of the past factors: initial application, sustained application, joy, happiness and one-pointedness of the mind that accompanied the first jhāna. If it follows after the fourth immaterial jhāna, the object is either equanimity or one-pointedness of the mind.

(4) The Path Process
(Magga Vīthi)

The cognitive process path is four-fold: the path of the stream enterer, of once returner, of non-returner and of an Arahant. Of them the process of the path of the stream enterer is also five-fold: the first, second, third, fourth and fifth jhāna process of the path of the stream enterer.

The first jhāna path of the stream enterer process is as follows: When the meditator is about to attain the path, one of the three characteristics of existence becomes clearly comprehended at the avenue of the mind-door, the bhavanga vibrates twice and is arrested, then arises mind-door adverting citta and then one of four sense-sphere wholesome cittas functions as the preliminary javanas. If the individual is dull-witted, this occurs four times: corresponding to the stages of preparation, access, conformity and change-of-lineage. Then, one javana and two fruition javanas arise. However, if the individual is keen-witted, it only occurs three times: corresponding to access, conformity and change-of-lineage. Then, one path javana and three fruition javanas arise, bhavangas are interrupted for some moments and this is followed by the reviewing processes of the path, the fruition, Nibbāna, the eradicated defilements and non-eradicated defilements.

Dull-Witted First Jhāna Stream Enterer Path Process

SB	"VB	AB	MA	PR	AC	CO	CL	MC	FC	FC"	SB
ooo	ooo	ooo	ooo	ooo	ooo	ooo	ooo	ooo	ooo	ooo	ooo

Keen-Witted First Jhāna Stream Enterer Path Process

SB	"VB	AB	MA	AC	CO	CL	MC	FC	FC	FC"	SB
ooo	ooo	ooo	ooo	ooo	ooo	ooo	ooo	ooo	ooo	ooo	ooo

Dull-Witted First Jhāna Higher Path Process

SB	"VB	AB	MA	PR	AC	CO	PF	PC	FC	FC"	SB
ooo	ooo	ooo	ooo	ooo	ooo	ooo	ooo	ooo	ooo	ooo	ooo

Keen-Witted First Jhāna Higher Path Process

SB	"VB	AB	MA	AC	CO	PF	PC	FC	FC	FC"	SB
ooo	ooo	ooo	ooo	ooo	ooo	ooo	ooo	ooo	ooo	ooo	ooo

Note: SB= Stream of bhavanga; VB= vibrating bhavanga; AB= arrested bhavanga; MA= mind-door adverting; PR= preparation; AC= access; CO= conformity; CL= change-of lineage; MC= the path cons; FC= fruition cons; PF= purification (vodāna).

Explanation

When one practises insight meditation (Vipassanā) on the conditioning states or on mental and material phenomenon, then, as meditation develops, one realizes the three characteristics of impermanence, suffering and non-self. One then reaches the supramundane paths and fruition. However, the meditators differ among themselves, in the degree of the development of their concentration. Those who develop insight, without the basis of jhāna, are called practitioners of bare insight (sukkhavipassaka). When they reach the path and fruition, their path and fruition cittas occur at a level corresponding to the first jhāna. Those who develop insight on the basis of jhāna, attain a path and fruit that corresponds to the level of jhāna they had attained before reaching the path[5]. Thus, there are two ways to reach the supramundane state: Vipassanā-yānika (i.e. via the practises of bare Vipassanā as the vehicle) and Samatha-yānika (i.e. via the practises of tranquillity meditation as the vehicle before Vipassanā). A meditator may first develop access concentration by practising tranquillity meditation and then proceed to Vipassanā. Thus, access concentration is the foundation for insight into one of the three characteristics; this will enable one to reach the state of path and fruition. Now consider the meditator who first develops a jhāna by tranquillity meditation and uses this jhāna as the foundation of his Vipassanā insight. If he uses the first jhāna as his foundation, his first path consciousness is also accompanied by the first jhāna and so is known as the first jhāna stream enterer process. Similarly, if a meditator uses the second, third, fourth or fifth jhāna as the foundation, his first path consciousness is accompanied by the respective jhāna. Therefore, the path of the stream enterer process is five-fold. Like-wise each of the remaining paths and fruition processes are also five fold.

Once a meditator becomes a noble one (ariya), through the arising of the path process, he never reverts back to being a worldling again; thus, change-of-lineage (gotrabhū) will not arise with the other path processes, instead purification (vodāna) will arise. In the case of the first path attainment, this moment is called "change-of-lineage" because it marks the transition from the lineage of a worldling to the lineage of the noble ones. This expression continues to be used figuratively as the change-of-lineage for the moment of transition to the higher paths. Sometimes, however, it is designated by the different name of vodāna meaning purification. This is because gradual purification of some defilements is extended and it takes Nibbāna as a truly pure object.

Three Theories

Those who develop Vipassanā insight, on the basis of jhāna, attain a path and fruition that correspond to the level of jhāna, which had been attained before realization of the path. The ancient teachers advance three different theories on the jhāna level of the path and fruition. One school of thought holds that, it is the basic jhāna (pādakaj jhāna) that is used as a basis for concentrating the mind before developing the insight, which culminates in attainment of the path. The second theory holds that, the jhāna level of the path is determined by the jhāna used as an object for investigation by insight; this is called comprehended or investigated jhāna (sammasitajjhāna). The third school of thought holds that, when a meditator has mastered a range of jhāna, he can choose the jhāna level of the path by his personal wish or inclination (puggalajjhāsaya). Nevertheless, no matter what explanation is adopted, it does not make much difference with regard to the process of the path and fruition.

Path and Reviewing Processes

There are four path processes, each has five jhānas, so there are twenty (4X5=20) in total. Multiplying by the two individuals, dull-witted or keen-witted, results in forty processes (20X2=40).

After each path process the reviewing processes follow. After the first path process, for example, there follows the reviewing of the path, fruition, Nibbāna, and the eradicated defilements and non-eradicated defilements; thus five reviewing processes follow. Likewise, the second and third path processes are followed by five reviewing processes. However, in the case of the fourth path, defilements have already been eradicated and so, only four reviewing processes occur.

Thus, there are essentially nineteen reviewing processes in total (3X5=15+4=19). In more detail, according to jhānic attainment, each path has five different processes. Therefore, there are twenty processes in total. Of these, the first, second and third path processes multiplied by five reviewing processes, yields seventy-five (15X5=75). As each of the fourth path jhānas is only followed four reviewing processes, it becomes twenty processes (5X4=20). Thus, ninety-five reviewing processes (75+20=95) in total follow after all the path processes.

Cittas and Object

The following cittas participate in the first jhāna process: 1 mind-door adverting, 2 sense-sphere javanas that are wholesome consciousnesses accompanied by joy associated with knowledge, 1 first path consciousness and 1 first fruition citta. Thus, there are five cittas in total. All cittas, except bhavanga and the one that functions as the change-of-lineage, have the object of conditioning states in the three realms. (This means all mental and material objects in the three worlds: sense-sphere, fine-material and immaterial realms). The citta functions of change-of-lineage, path and fruition, have Nibbāna as their object.

Plane and Individuals

This first jhāna stream enterer path process arises in seven sensuous blissful realms and ten fine-material realms, except for the five pure abodes. It arises in three types of individual: the worldling whose rebirth consciousness is triple rooted, the individual who has achieved the stream enterer path and its fruition. In fact, the moment of mind-door citta, the moment of sense-sphere javana: preparation, access, conformity and change-of-lineage arises in the worldling, the moment path javana arises in the stream enterer path individual and the moment fruition javana arises in the individual who has attained that fruition state; these processes occur in the sense-sphere and fine-material realms. Thus, the four sense-sphere triple rooted resultant cittas and the five fine-material resultant cittas function as bhavangas.

Higher Jhāna and Path Processes

One should understand that the second to fifth jhāna, higher jhāna and stream enterer processes and their cittas, objects, planes and individuals are very similar to the first jhāna stream enterer process. However, one should note that, in the fifth jhāna path process the preliminary sense-sphere javanas (i.e. preparatory, access, conformity and change-of-lineage) that arise, prior to the path, function by two sense-sphere wholesome consciousness accompanied by equanimity and associated with knowledge. Likewise, all path and fruition javana cittas function by their respective cittas. The second and third path processes are found in the seven sensuous blissful planes, ten fine-material and four immaterial realms. The Arahanta path process also arises in the five pure abodes. Depending on the realm, the bhavanga cittas function as one of the four sense-sphere triple rooted cittas or one of the nine sublime cittas. With respect to individuals, the triple rooted worldling individual who has achieved the first path will go on to achieve the first fruition and only they can achieve the second path. Therefore, the path of once returner process arises in the three types of individuals: one who has achieved stream enterer fruition, one who has attained the path of once returning and one has attained its fruition.

Amongst the reviewing processes, these processes, which review the path, the fruition and Nibbāna, are eight sense-sphere wholesome and functional cittas associated with knowledge. When reviewing the eradicated and non-eradicated defilements, the sixteen sense-sphere wholesome and functional cittas function as javana. The object of these processes is the same as that which they review. Regarding the individual, wholesome cittas arise in trainees but only functional cittas arise in Arahanta. Only those who have achieved fruition are capable of reviewing, and therefore, the reviewing process arises only in the four noble ones.

(5) The Fruition Process (Phalasamāpatti Vīthi)

Entering Attainment of Fruition Process

The process of entering fruition, like the path process, is also fivefold according to the different levels of jhāna. The process of entering the first jhāna fruition occurs as follows. The stream enterer, who has attained the first jhāna, the path and fruition, would then like to live experiencing the fruition of his attainment. By taking Nibbāna as an object, he meditates on the conditioning states of mental and material phenomenon. When one of the three characteristics of the phenomenal world enters very clearly at the avenue of his mind-door, bhavanga vibrates twice and is arrested. A mind-door adverting citta arises. Then, if the individual is dull-witted, conformity arises four times as preliminary javana. If he is keen-witted, conformity arises only three times as preliminary javana. Then, fruition javanas arise for as long the meditator wishes. When he emerges from the fruition process there follows subsidence into the bhavanga stream.

In the same way, one must understand the remaining process of entering fruition stages accordingly.

Dull-Witted Individual Entering First Jhāna Stream Enterer Fruition Process

SB	"VB	AB	MA	CO	CO	CO	CO	FJ	...	..."	SB
000	000	000	000	000	000	000	000	000	000	000	000

Keen-Witted First Jhāna Stream Enterer Fruition Process

SB	"VB	AB	MA	CO	CO	CO	FJ	...	..."	SB
000	000	000	000	000	000	000	000	000	000	000

Note: FJ= fruition javana
...= fruition javana (as long as)

Explanation

There are four noble individuals: the stream enterer, the once returner, the non-returner and the Arahanta. Each of the noble ones may enter the respective fruition process, according to his attainment. Just as a king experiences royal bliss and a deva (or deity) experiences divine bliss, so too the noble ones abide experiencing nibbānic bliss here and now. The object of the fruition citta is Nibbāna. Therefore, entering the fruition process means experiencing the bliss of Nibbāna. A noble one can live in this state for as long as he wishes, up to a maximum of seven days. Thus, living with the Nibbānic peace that corresponds to the subsequent arising of fruition javanas, is called entering the fruition state. Likewise, subsidence into the bhavanga is called emerging from the fruition process.

According to ancient tradition, there are one hundred and twenty different entering fruition processes. However, we count only forty different processes, as explained in our description of the path process. These processes can also occur in the sensuous realm, and in the fine-material and immaterial realms. However, it should be noted that the stream enterer and once returning fruition processes can not occur in the five pure abodes. All bhavanga functions for this person are one of thirteen triple bhavanga cittas, this means four wholesome resultant cittas associate with knowledge and nine fine-material and immaterial resultant cittas.

Conformity javana, in the first three fruitions, function as one of the wholesome cittas associated with knowledge, and in the Arahanta, fruition functions as one of the functional cittas associated with knowledge. If the fifth jhāna citta is accompanied by equanimity, and if other lower jhāna citta are accompanied by joy or equanimity, one should understand this according to the level of jhāna, the individual and the fruition stages.

Conformity-Anuloma

The name of the preliminary javana prior to the fruition javana is conformity (anuloma). It is said in the Paṭṭhāna[6]: "arahato anulomaṁ phalasamāpattiyā anantara paccayena paccayo, sekkhānaṁ anulomaṁ phalasamāpattiyā anantara paccayena paccayo." However, in the "Path of Purification", Ācariya Buddhaghosa named it as change-of-lineage (gotrabhū).

Conformity javana, prior to fruition javana, does not take Nibbāna as an object unlike the change-of-lineage, prior to the path javana. However, the object of conformity is the conditioning state of mental and material phenomenon. Of course, the function of the path is to emancipate beings, to free them from the round of suffering. Therefore, the change-of-lineage prior to the path does not take the conditioning states as an object; instead it takes Nibbāna as an object in accordance with the path. On the other hand, the function of the fruition cittas is not to emancipate as such, but to experience the Nibbānic peace here and now. Therefore, conformity javana cittas, prior to fruition, have no need to leave the conditioning states as an object. Thus, conformity javanas prior to the fruition javana do not take Nibbāna as an object but take the conditioning states as the object. This is unlike the change-of-lineage (or purification) prior to the path[7].

Two or three fruition javanas arise in the path process, however, this is not a state of entering fruition absorption; rather they arise as the result of the path javana. To enter the fruition state one has to practice preliminary meditation without the path; by observing the conditioning states as impermanence, suffering and non-self. Thus, the arising of fruition javanas, without the path, is called entering the fruition state. Before entering the fruition states, one has to make a determination regarding the amount of time one will stay in this state (up to a maximum of seven days). When this determined time is completed, the fruition javana process ceases and the bhavanga citta arises. The occurring of bhavanga, at the end of the fruition javana, is called the emerging from the fruition process.

(6) **Direct Knowledge Process**
(Abhiññā Vīthi)

The direct knowledge process is seven-fold: (i) various supernormal powers process, (ii) the divine ear, (iii) the ability to read the minds of others, (iv) the ability to remember former existences, (v) the divine eye, (vi) the knowledge of (beings) faring according to their deeds and (vii) the knowledge of future processes. Of these, the various supernormal powers process is three-fold[8]: (i) the success by resolve process, (ii) the success as a transformation process and (iii) success as mind-made process.

The direct knowledge of the success by resolve process runs as follows: Generally, for one who is accomplished in the eight attainments of absorption, if he wants to produce various powers, at first he observes one of the kasiṇa objects and enters the absorption state process. This is the basic absorption process for the direct knowledge. Then, if he wishes to make himself manifold, he makes a determination such as "let there be a hundred or a thousand identical but separate forms of myself." Then the preliminary action sense-sphere-javana mind-door processes runs; this is the basic process needed to succeed in his resolution. Then, again observing one of the kasiṇa objects, he enters the fine-material fifth jhāna attainment process; this is a basic process of direct knowledge. Then, observing a hundred or a thousand forms, there runs a direct knowledge process that enables him to produce the many forms that he has resolved to create. Spontaneously various supernormal powers appear, according to his resolution.

Basic Jhāna Process

SB	"VB	AB	MA	PR	AC	CO	CL	JC	JC	JC"	SB
000	000	000	000	000	000	000	000	000	000	000	000

Preliminary Action Process

SB	"VB	AB	MA	JC	JC	JC	JC	JC	JC	JC"	SB
000	000	000	000	000	000	000	000	000	000	000	000

Abhiññā Process

SB	"VB	AB	MA	PR	AC	CO	CL	DK"	SB
000	000	000	000	000	000	000	000	000	000

Note: DK= Direct Knowledge (Abhiññā)

Explanation

The special force of knowledge that is associated with the fine-material fifth jhāna wholesome and the functional consciousness is direct knowledge. Thus the whole fine-material fifth jhāna is designated as abhiññā, or direct knowledge. The process of direct knowledge (abhiññā) is seven-fold as follows:-

(i) Iddhividha abhiññā: The power of creating forms, flying through the air, walking on water, diving into the earth and so on.
(ii) Dibbasota abhiññā: The divine ear, which enables one to hear subtle or coarse sounds far or near.
(iii) Paracittavijānana: The power of penetrating the minds of others to discern their thoughts.
(iv) Pubbenivāsānussati: The power to remember one's former existences and the former worlds in which one has lived.
(v) Dibba-cakkhu: The divine eye, which enables one to see subtle or

coarse things far or near and also, the celestial worlds and the woeful planes.

(vi) Yathākammūpaga ñāṇa: The power of seeing beings in the 31 planes of existence and knowing their respective kammas, which have given rise to their rebirths.

(vii) Anāgataṁsa ñāṇa: The power of knowing future existences and future worlds.

The fine-material jhānas are enumerated as four and immaterial jhānas are also four. Thus, it is said, "there are eight attainments of absorption." One who wishes to attain direct knowledge must be accomplished in all eight jhānic states. This person should not only have attained the eight jhānic attainments but also, he must be the master of these attainments. For the path of purification, Visuddhimagga says "He must achieve the eight attainments in each of the eight kasiṇas (earth, water, fire, air, blue, yellow, red and white). He must also have complete control of his mind in the following fourteen ways: (i) in the order of the kasiṇa, (ii) in the reverse order of the kasiṇa, (iii) in the order and reverse order of the kasiṇa, (iv) in the order of the jhānas, (v) in the reverse order of the jhānas, (vi) in the order and reverse order of the jhānas, (vii) skipping jhānas, (viii) skipping kasiṇas, (ix) skipping jhānas and kasiṇas (x) transposition of factors, (xi) transposition of object, (xii) transposition of factors and object, (xiii) definition of factors and (xiv) definition of object." However, for those whose wisdom is very sharp, or who have acute insight, following the attainment of the fifth jhāna, or the path and fruition insight, they attain direct knowledge spontaneously[9].

One who has direct knowledge and wishes to perform supernormal powers at first enters the basic jhānic process and the preliminary action process. Then, he enters the basic process of the fifth jhāna and then enters the process of abhiññā, supernormal powers. There is no definite number of jhānas in the basic jhāna process. This is a kind of entry into jhānic attainment: jhāna may arise as much as necessary and then there follows the processes of reviewing of the jhānic factors as usual.

What is the benefit of entering the basic jhānic absorption processes? For one who enters the basic absorption processes, his samādhi (concentration) becomes very strong. This enables him to establish preliminary action. He resolves, "Let there be a hundred or a thousand identical but separate forms of myself." His mind is steady towards the object that he is resolving. Thus, entering the basic jhānic absorption process is essential.

Here the words "let there be a hundred or a thousand" are not to be chanted repeatedly. Rather, this is an expression of the aspiration of one's resolve. Therefore, this process is also called "resolving process"; and it is a sensuous javana mind-door process. This process may have to occur many times in order to fulfil the aspiration. Then, the meditator again enters the fifth jhāna process that is basis the of the abhiññā process. Why does one have to enter again the fifth jhāna process, that is the basis of abhiññā process? The reason is that one needs to enter again the basic process in order to make one's resolution powerful. Thus, in order to have a strong abhiññā one has to enter the basic process. For those whose direct knowledge is natural, and for whom it has become habitual for them, the basic process may not be necessary. Therefore, Ācariya Anuruddha and other commentators do not mention the last basic jhāna process.

As long as the direct knowledge process does not arise, many basic jhāna processes and preliminary action processes will be run again and again. This process cannot occur in the immaterial realm because there is no entering of the fifth fine-material jhāna process. However, it does occur in the seven sensuous blissful planes and the fifteen fine-material realms. Therefore, one of four sense-sphere triple rooted cittas, or the five fine-material resulting cittas, participate as bhavanga accordingly. These direct knowledge processes arise in the five types of individuals: the triple rooted worldling and the four noble ones. The functional abhiññās occur in the Arahant, and the wholesome abhiññās occur in the triple rooted worldling and the three trainee types. The javana cittas prior to abhiññā must be the sense-sphere wholesome and functional cittas accompanied by equanimity, i.e. they must be consistent with the fine-material fifth jhāna. If the individual is keen-witted, the preliminary javana arise only three times.

We have explained briefly the basic direct knowledge process (abhiññā), its basic processes and preliminary action processes. The other direct knowledge processes for different supernormal powers are the same, except in regard to the preliminary action processes[10].

(7) Entering into the Attainment of Cessation Process (Nirodha-samāpatti Vīthi)

Consider two types of noble ones: a non-returner and an Arahant, who are accomplished in the eight jhānic attainments, in sense-sphere and fine-material plane, who see the five-aggregates of the body and mental states as a burden, are disgusted with them, and would like to live experiencing the bliss of Nibbāna here and now. At first these types of individual enter the mundane first jhānic state. They then meditate on the jhānic consciousness and its factors, observing their impermanence, suffering and non-self nature. Then, in the same way, they enter the second, third and fourth jhāna of fine-material, and then the first and second jhāna of immaterial states, one by one. Whenever they emerge from each jhānic state, they observe its respective consciousness and its factors, as impermanent, suffering and non-self. They enter the third immaterial jhānic state, and emerge from it; but they do not observe or meditate on the jhāna consciousness and its factors. Instead there occur four kinds of preparatory tasks of sensuous javana mind-door processes: resolving non-danger to other property (nānābaddha avikopana), Sangha's waiting (sangha paṭimānana), the Buddha's summons (satthupakkosana) and the limit of the life duration (addhānaparicccheda). Then, they enter the fourth immaterial jhāna, i.e. the neither perception nor-non-perception state. After two jhāna moments, they enter the attainment of cessation with the ceasing of consciousness, mental concomitants (cetasika) and mind-born matters[11]. When they emerge from the cessation state, one fruition javana arises. If the individual is a non-returner, non-returner fruition or an Arahant, the arahatta fruition javana arises. Then, there is subsidence into the bhavanga stream.

The Attainment of Cessation Process

SB	"VB	AB	MA	PR	AC	CO	CL	JC	JC	Cessation	FC"	SB
ooo	ooo	ooo	ooo	ooo	ooo	ooo	ooo	ooo	ooo	......	ooo	ooo

Explanation

There are only two types of noble ones who are able to enter the attainment of cessation: the non-returner and Arahant who have attained the eight jhānic states. The attainment of cessation process is attained by the power of tranquillity (samatha), meditation and insight (vipassanā) meditation. The attainment of cessation is the non-occurrence of consciousness and its mental concomitants owing to their progressive cessation. The person who wants to attain this process at first has to achieve all the jhānic states and practice vipassanā meditation. He must observe the jhānic consciousnesses and their factors as impermanent, suffering and non-self. Thus, developing both samatha and vipassanā together, one can attain the cessation state. Note that, in the immaterial realm this process cannot occur because there is no fine-material jhāna which can be attained. However, this process can occur in the sensuous blissful plane and fine-material plane.

Fourfold Resolution

The noble one, just before he enters the state of cessation, makes these fourfold resolutions:

(i) Non-danger to other property (nānābaddha avikopana): Before one enters into the state of cessation, one should resolve that "such and such other property should not be damaged or destroyed by fire, water, winds, thieves and so on." Those requisites, inner and outer robes, as he sits facing east, which are with him, cannot be destroyed by the power of his attainment. The other properties, such as, a bowl, bed, chair, living room, or any other kinds of various requisites belonging to him or to others, can be destroyed during his state of cessation. Therefore, he makes this resolution before he enters the state of cessation.

(ii) Sangha's waiting (sangha paṭimānana): The Sangha may be waiting for him to perform the Sangha's acts. So, he makes the resolution, "While I am sitting for seven days in the attainment of cessation, if the Sangha needs me, I will emerge from the state of cessation." This resolution makes him able to emerge from the cessation state, before any monk comes to call him. If he does not make this resolution, the Sangha may send a monk to summon him. As soon as the monk calls his name, he will emerge from the cessation state.

(iii) The Buddha's summons (satthupakkosana): He makes the resolution that "If the Buddha needs me for any reason, I will emerge from the cessation state before someone comes and summons me." This resolution enables him to emerge from the cessation state before someone comes to summon him. However, if he does not make this resolution before his entering the cessation state, he will emerge as soon as someone summons him.

(iv) The limit of the life duration (addhānaparicceheda): He should be very careful to determine what the limit of his life's duration is. However, if his life's duration is within the seven days of his attainment of cessation, he has to emerge from the cessation state before the time of his death. If he were to die at the moment of emerging from the cessation state, he will (in the case of non-returner) have missed his opportunity to practice for Arahantship. If he is an Arahanta, he has no time to inform the Sangha of his attainment of Arahantship and to give guidance to the Sangha. This resolution is therefore most essential, and he must make it before entering the cessation state. The rest are not essential.

In this process, jhāna is the fourth jhāna of the immaterial plane that is neither perception nor non-perception. If the individual is a non-returner, the wholesome jhāna and the non-returner fruition citta occur. If the individual is an Arahant, the functional jhāna and arahatta fruition citta occur. Sense-sphere wholesome and functional cittas accompanied by equanimity; and associated with knowledge, function as preliminary javana etc[12]; prior to the equanimity jhāna. Four sense-sphere triple cittas, and five fine-material resultant cittas, function as bhavanga in the seven sense-sphere state and the five material states. The attainment of cessation is the benefit gained from the wisdom of the noble path. In vipassanā (insight) the attainment of fruition is the benefit. Direct knowledge is the outcome of mundane concentration, samādhi.

Why do only two jhānas arise before the attainment of cessation? The reason is that all preliminary efforts are just for the attainment of cessation. For example, before the attainment of cessation one has to make a great effort to attain the first jhāna and so on. The development of both samatha and vipassanā meditation, in each of the jhānic stages, is not for the attainment of the neither perception nor non-perception jhāna; rather their development is only for the attainment of cessation. Therefore, in the process of the neither perception nor non-perception, after two jhāna moments, one enters the attainment of cessation state[13].

The stream enterer and the once returner cannot achieve the attainment of cessation. This is because they have not eradicated the latent tendency of sensuous desire. This is the major hindrance to concentration, and their concentration is still weak. On the other hand, the non-returner and Arahant have up-rooted the latent tendency of sensuous desire; therefore, their concentration (samādhi) is extremely strong and sufficient for them to enter the attainment of cessation. Whenever they observe the rising and passing away of conditioning states, they feel dissatisfied or disgusted with them, and wish to live peacefully, free from the conditioning states, and enter the attainment of cessation.

When one eats food, one can be sustained for seven days in the sensuous plane; likewise one can remain in the attainment of cessation state for seven days at most. Sensuous plane means the human realm, the other higher sensuous blissful realms are also full of various sense pleasures and it is difficult to find a place of solitude in them. Therefore, a non-returner will be reborn in the jhānic realm, or in the pure abodes, after which they may become Arahant and achieve Parinibbāna.

What is the difference between one who is dead and one who has achieved the attainment of cessation? When a person is dead, he has completed his life span. His bodily formations, verbal formations and mental formations have ceased and are quite still. His life is exhausted, his heat has subsided and his faculties are broken up. On the other hand, when a person enters the attainment of cessation his bodily formations, verbal formations and mental formations have ceased and are quite still but his life is un-exhausted, his temperature has not subsided and his faculties are quite whole.

The attainment of cessation is not classified as a conditioning state or un-conditioned state, or mundane or supra-mundane. This is because it has no essence as reality. However, since this state of cessation is attained by a person making great effort then, if it were to be classified, it would be regarded as produced (nipphanna), not un-produced (anipphanna)[14].

(8) Dying Process
(Maraṇāsanna Vīthi)

Five Sense-Door Dying Process

The dying process is twofold: the five sense door process and the mind door process. The five sense door process is further subdivided into five different processes: the eye-door, ear-door, nose-door, tongue-door and the body-door process. Of these the eye-door process has four types: death consciousness arising after javana, death consciousness arising after javana and bhavanga, death consciousness arising after registration and death consciousness arising after registration and bhavanga. The process in which death consciousness arises after javana occurs as follows:

> When a visible object appears to a dying person's eye after one bhavanga has passed, it enters the avenue of the eye; the bhavanga citta vibrates for two thought moments and is arrested. Then, five-door adverting consciousness arises and ceases adverting to that same visible object. Immediately after there arises and ceases in due order: eye-consciousness seeing that object, receiving consciousness receiving it, investigating consciousness investigating it and determining consciousness determining it. Following this any one of the twenty-nine sense-sphere dying javana cittas runs for five thought moments. After the javanas there arises the death consciousness. This is followed by re-birth consciousness. Then, fifteen or sixteen bhavanga cittas arise accordingly and then a mind-door adverting citta, followed by seven existence-craving (bhava-nikantika) javana cittas. Then comes the subsidence into the bhavanga (life-continuum) stream.

The Dying Process Death Consciousness Arises after Javana

IG	DC	JC	JC	JC	JC	JC	CC	PC	BC	SB	"PB	VB	AB	FA	EC	RC	BC	BC	BC
ooo	ooo	ooo	ooo	ooo	ooo	ooo	ooo	ooo	ooo	ooo	ooo	ooo	ooo	ooo	ooo	ooo	ooo	ooo	ooo
BC	BC	BC	BC	MA	JC	JC	JC	JC	JC	BC	BC	BC	BC	BC	BC	BC	JC	JC"	SB
ooo	ooo	ooo	ooo	ooo	ooo	ooo	ooo	ooo	ooo	ooo	ooo	ooo	ooo	ooo	ooo	ooo	ooo	ooo	ooo

Note: ooo= the three minor instants of arising, existing and dissolution of one thought moment. SB= stream of bhavanga; PB= past bhavanga; VB= vibrating bhavanga; AB= arrest bhavanga; FA= five-door adverting; EC= eye consciousness; RV= receiving; IG= investigating; DC= determining cons; JC= javana cons; RS= registration; CC= cuti (death) consciousness, PC= paṭisandhi (rebirth) consciousness, BC= bhavanga cons, MA= mind-door adverting cons

Explanation

Any cognitive process which at the end (with or without interrupting bhavangas) causes the death consciousness to arise is called a "dying process". Ancient teachers of the Abhidhamma did not mention the rebirth process separately but included it within the dying process. So, here both the dying and rebirth cognitive process are explained briefly.

The dying process described above occurs with a very great object. Three conditions are present in this process: sense-sphere javana, sense-sphere being and sense-sphere realm. However, registration is arising. When kamma-born matters have ceased the death consciousness will arise. Also, for the person whose birth citta is accompanied by equanimity, the object is very desirable and javana is accompanied with displeasure; in this situation, without registration as shown above, the death citta arises.

With the process where the death citta arises after javana and bhavanga, the bhavanga citta arises not only for one moment but two, three or more moments will be arising as long as kamma-born matters have not ceased. For those whose birth citta is accompanied with equanimity, the object is very desirable and javana is accompanied with displeasure; for them this kind of process will occur. Also, for those whose birth citta was accompanied by joy, but javana was accompanied by displeasure for them with transitional bhavanga, the process occurs. Not only with a very great object, but also with a great object process, the death citta arises after javana. One should understand that similar processes occur with the other sense objects relating to the five sense-doors.

In this five-door dying process there occur 54 sense-sphere cittas. Excluded are the 9 functional javanas, since functional javanas occur only in Arahants; though Arahants do not attain Nibbāna with five sense-door processes. The preceding existence's bhavangas and death citta take as object kamma, the sign of kamma or the sign of destiny, which is the object of the past existence's javana. However, the last phrase, i.e. "which is the object of the past existence's javana", is still unclear.

As well as bhavanga and death cittas, other cittas occur in the process, e.g. the five-door adverting cittas etc. These take one of the five sense objects of kamma, the sign of kamma or the sign of destiny as their objects. Indeed, the object of the dying process is named one of kamma, sign of kamma or sign of destiny. Kamma means the volition through which one performed good or bad deeds in the past but during the same life time. Therefore, the five sense objects cannot be called kamma. The sign of destiny is a symbol of the realm into which the dying person is about to be reborn and so, some teachers say that this sign of destiny cannot appear in the five sense-door process; it can only appear in the mind-door process. The sign of kamma means an object or image associated with the good or evil deed that is about to determine rebirth or else an instrument that has been used to perform it. This sign is the main cause of successful kamma[15]; it is therefore called the sign of kamma. This sign or instrument is one of the sense objects. The five sense-door process takes only the present sense object, therefore it is said "the process takes the present five sense object of the sign of kamma as its object."

The rebirth citta and the bhavanga cittas, in the new existence, also take the five sense object of the sign of kamma as their object but distinguishing between the present and past sign of kamma is dependent on the process. The following example illustrates this point. From the past bhavanga to the death citta, if the sense object has not completed seventeen mind moments of its life time, then the rebirth citta and some bhavanga cittas have the present sense object of the sign of kamma as their object; and the next bhavanga citta takes the past sense object as the sign of kamma. If the object of the preceding existence has completed seventeen mind moments at the death moment, the rebirth citta and other bhavanga cittas take the past sense object as the sign of kamma. Thus, one should understand the object of rebirth and bhavanga cittas in the new existence.

A mind-door adverting citta, and seven javanas of existence-craving cittas take the object of mental resultant aggregates and kamma-born matters (kaṭattā) called rebirth-linking (paṭisandhi). (Resultant cittas that perform re-linking, their associate cetasikas and kamma- born matters that arise together with them are called paṭisandhi). For example, wholesome resultant first citta, its associate 33 cetasikas and 3 kamma-born kalāpa are called "triple rooted paṭisandhi[16]". This rebirth-linking (paṭisandhi) is also called bhava (becoming or process of existence) and the javana cittas crave them as their object (i.e. craving for existence). Therefore, these are called "existence-craving javanas (bhavanikantika javana)." (This is common for all living beings, whether their rebirth is in blissful realms or in woeful realms. They have attachment to their own becoming or life).

At the time of death, kamma-born material phenomena (kalāpas) no longer arise after the seventeenth consciousness preceding the death consciousness. Therefore, the sense consciousnesses (eye, ear etc.), unlike in the course of existence processes, have their base in the five sense bases that arise at the instant of the arising of the seventeenth consciousness preceding death consciousness. It is possible that the five sense consciousnesses are based on any base, which is present at the moment of their arising. Like-wise, other cittas (except sense consciousnesses) also arise in the heart base that arises with the seventeenth citta preceding the death citta. As in the course of existence process, there is no heart base that arises with each preceding citta.

The new rebirth linking citta, in this present existence, has no heart base that arises with the preceding citta; therefore, it is based on the heart base that arises together with it. Bhavanga, mind-door adverting and javana cittas are based on the heart base that arises with their respective preceding cittas. For example, the first bhavanga after the rebirth citta is based on the heart base that arises together with rebirth citta, and so on.

These five sense-door processes occur in the sense-sphere and fine-material plane for those who have died in the sense-sphere plane and will be reborn again in the sense-sphere plane. This also occurs for those who have died in the fine-material plane and will be born in the sense-sphere plane. (Note that, the person who dies in the fine-material plane and is reborn in the sense-sphere plane will not have nose, tongue and body processes because these three sense-doors do not exist in that plane, and also registration will not arise). The five sense-door processes will not occur, in those who will be reborn in the fine-material and immaterial realms. This is because the sign of kamma object of the person who will be born in those realms is the earth kasiṇa etc[17].

The person taking rebirth from the immaterial realm to the sense-sphere plane will have no object of material phenomena. Therefore, the five sense-door processes will not occur there because he couldn't take material phenomena as an object. These processes occur in six individuals: four worldlings, the stream-enterer and the once returner. These processes will not occur in the non-returner or Arahants[18], since they will not be reborn in the sense-sphere plane at all.

Mind-Door Dying Process

There are two types of mind-door dying process: the worldling and trainee's dying process and the Arahant's dying process. Of these the worldling and trainee's dying process (where the person is taking rebirth in the sense-sphere plane) is of four kinds, as in the sense-door process. These are: the process in which the death citta arises after javana, after javana and bhavanga, after registration, and after registration and bhavanga. If the person dies in the sense-sphere plane, and takes rebirth in other planes, only two kinds of processes occur: the process in which the death citta arises after javana or the process in which the death citta arises after javana and bhavanga. The same applies if the person dies in other planes and takes rebirth in the sense-sphere plane.

Explanation

Consider the person who has died in the sense-sphere plane and takes rebirth in the same sense-sphere plane. For this person, if the three conditions of sense-sphere javana, sense-sphere being and clear object exist, then the dying process will occur with registration. If the object is obscure, but death is very near, registration will not arise. The same applies even for a sense-sphere clear object. Thus, four kinds of process occur in the worldling's and trainee's dying process. Consider the person who has died in the sense-sphere plane and is taking rebirth in the other planes (fine-material and immaterial). Though there is a sense-sphere javana, and a sense-sphere being, registration cannot arise. As the objects of the rebirth citta, of the fine-material and immaterial realms, are either concept or sublime accordingly, then the person who is taking rebirth in these realms, from the sense-sphere plane, must also have that object of concept or sublime, and in these cases registration cannot arise. For the person who has died in other realms, and is taking rebirth in the sense-sphere plane, they are not a sense-sphere being and so registration cannot arise. Therefore, if the person has died in the sense-sphere plane and takes rebirth in other planes, for them only two kinds of processes occur. The same applies for the person who died in other planes and takes rebirth in the sense-sphere plane.

These processes have various objects: past or present sense-sphere, sublime and concept. Of these, the object is the present sign of kamma, or destiny of kamma. If the death citta arises after javana, there are ten citta moments, from the past bhavanga to the death citta. Therefore, the rebirth citta and six bhavanga cittas after rebirth, take the same present sense object. Also, is "destiny of kamma" the correct term to use? In the case of the mind-door dying process (except the dying process of Arahants) there are 32 sense-sphere cittas. Excluded from these are 10 sense consciousnesses, 3 mind element cittas that occur exclusively in the five sense-doors and 9 functional javanas that only occur in Arahants. For those who are taking rebirth in the fine-material realm, the object is a concept, which is the sign of kamma. In the immaterial realm, the object is a sublime state or a concept of a sign of kamma accordingly. For those who are taking rebirth in the sense-sphere realm, the object is a sense-object of kamma, a sign of kamma or a sign of destiny. For more details see *A Comprehensive*

Manual of Abhidhamma.

These processes occur in all realms except the realm of non-percipient beings and in seven individuals: four worldlings and three trainees accordingly.

Bhavanga Process

There are nineteen cittas that function as bhavanga. They are: two rootless decision cittas accompanied by equanimity, eight sense-sphere resultants, five fine-material resultants and four immaterial resultants. Among these only one of the cittas functions as bhavanga and this applies throughout the whole life time of the person. Which citta this is depends on the individual, the plane and other circumstances. Therefore, in this procedure there are certain planes, certain kinds of death and certain types of rebirth citta. These factors determine which citta functions as bhavanga in the preceding life and which functions as bhavanga in a new existence. One should understand that in a particular life rebirth, bhavanga and death cittas are similar and have an identical object. Therefore, we will explain here the relationship between the preceding death citta and the immediately following succeeding rebirth citta. This explanation will help students to understand not only bhavanga but also how one takes rebirth from one plane to another plane.

Following one of two rootless, and four double rooted preceding death citta, there occurs one of ten sense-sphere rebirth citta. The rootless and double rooted individual, who did not attain any jhānic states, will take rebirth in the sense-sphere plane. This will be with one of ten cittas: two rootless and eight sense-sphere resultant. Therefore, in the dying process of the preceding life, the bhavanga is performed by one of two rootless and four double rooted cittas, and in the new existence by one of ten sense-sphere bhavangas (2+8=10).

In the case of triple rooted worldlings, after one of four sense-sphere death cittas, rebirth occurs with one of nineteen rebirth cittas and one material rebirth, of non-percipience being[19]. In the case of the noble ones, after one of four sense-sphere death cittas, there occurs rebirth by one of four sense-sphere triple cittas or one of the nine material and immaterial cittas (4+9=13).

Now consider the death of a non-percipient being. Since he would have been unable to attain any jhānic states, he will not take rebirth in the fine-material or immaterial realms. However, by the power of access jhāna, he may take sense-sphere double rooted rebirth. So, in the case of a non-percipient being, death is followed by one of four sense-sphere double rooted cittas or one of four triple rooted rebirth cittas. Now consider the case of a worldling, after the occurrence of one of five death cittas. In the ten fine-material realms, from the first to the fourth jhāna realm of Great Reward (vehapphala) there follows one of seventeen rooted rebirth cittas: eight sensuous resultant and nine sublime resultants (8+9=17). Consider a noble one, who experiences one of four death cittas (except the fifth jhāna resultant) in the nine lower fine-material realms, up to the realm of Steady Aura (Subhakiṇha). Since one can again take rebirth in one's residing realm, there may follow rebirth citta of nine sublime resultant cittas in any of the upper realms of fine-material and immaterial rebirth. The noble ones, in jhānic realms, will not take rebirth in the lower realms. (Brahmalokagatā heṭṭhā ariyā nopapjjare)[20]

When Brahmas in the realm of Great Reward die, they will not take rebirth in any other plane. They may not achieve Arahantship because their five mental faculties of confidence, effort, awareness, concentration and wisdom may not be fully developed and in this case they may be reborn again in that realm. The realm of Great Reward and the realm of neither perception nor non-perception are the summit of the realms, from these realms the Brahmas will not take rebirth in any other realm. A person who dies in the Pure Abodes is a noble one, either a non-returner or an Arahant. The non-returner will not take rebirth in the same realm but instead will take rebirth in one of the upper realms. Therefore, after the death citta of pure abode occurs there is only rebirth via the pure abode fifth jhāna. For those who die in the highest pure abode, there is no succeeding rebirth because they are Arahants and for them there is no more rebirth.

If a worldling dies in the immaterial realm, he can again take rebirth in this realm or he may take rebirth in one of the upper realms. He may also take the triple rebirth in the sense-sphere plane. Therefore, after death there occurs rebirth via one of the four triple cittas or one of the four immaterial resultant cittas. (4+4=8) If a noble one dies in one of these realms, rebirth may occur in the same realm, or in one of the upper realms, via the four immaterial resultants.

Thus, one should understand all dying processes by studying the preceding death citta and the succeeding rebirth cittas, as applied to the respective individuals and planes.

Parinibbāna Process
(Parinibbāna Vīthi)

The Parinibbāna process, if it occurs in the sensuous javana mind-door process, is fourfold: the process in which the parinibbānic cessation occurs after javana; or after javana and bhavanga; or after registration; or after registration and bhavanga. If the cessation occurs in the sublime javanas process, there are four further processes: (i) jhāna contiguity process, (ii) reviewing contiguity process, (iii) abhiññā contiguity process and (iv) jīvita-samasīsī contiguity process[21].

Explanation

Parinibbāna Process (Sukkha-vipassaka): Consider a person who did not achieve any jhānic states but attained arahantship through Vipassanā only. Alternatively, suppose he achieved jhānic states but without entering the jhānic absorption states. For both these kind of person the parinibbānic cessation occurs at the end of the sense javana mind-door process. For this kind of Arahant the parinibbānic process is the same as the mind-door dying process, which has been described above. However, after parinibbānic cessation there is no rebirth process because all taints have been eradicated and so, they will have no more rebirths.

The object of cittas in the parinibbānic cessation process is unlike other dying processes. The parinibbānic cessation process may have as object (for example) mind-door adverting or registration, or any one of the mental and material objects and concepts in the triple planes (sensuous, fine-material and immaterial). There will be no resultant of kamma for future existences and there will be no destiny either. Therefore, kamma, the sign of kamma and the sign of destiny will not arise as the object of dying process cittas. Instead, one of the normal mundane mental or material phenomena or concepts appears as an object; and the cittas in the parinibbānic cessation process will take one of them as the object of the process. However, the parinibbānic cessation citta itself takes the same object (kamma, sign of kamma or sign of destiny) that was taken by the rebirth citta of the present existence. This is described in Chapter 5 of *A Comprehensive Manual of Abhidhamma* as follows: "rebirth consciousness, bhavanga citta and decease citta in one particular life are similar and have an identical object."

Now consider one who has attained the jhānic states. If this person ceased or entered into parinibbāna at the end of jhānic attainment, there would appear the respective object of kasiṇa concept etc. that was being used as the object of jhāna. This means that the jhāna cittas are dying javanas and the object of jhāna is the object of the dying javana. If one enters into parinibbāna after emerging from the jhānic states, and at the end of the reviewing of the jhānic factors, then the reviewing jhānic factors are the dying javanas and the jhānic factors are the object of dying javanas. If one enters into parinibbāna cessation at the end of the direct knowledge process, then the kamma-born body (i.e. the object of direct knowledge) appears as the object. The jīvitasamasīsī arahant enters into parinibbāna cessation after the arahatta path process and reviewing process; in this case it is the path and fruition that is the object of the reviewing process and which appear as the object of dying javanas. Thus, dying javanas preceding the parinibbānic cessation citta have as object one of mental phenomena, material phenomenon or concept. However, the parinibbānic cessation citta itself takes as its object the same object that was the object of rebirth citta in the present existence.

However, the Vibhāvanī Sub-commentary[22] states that (according to some teachers) the parinibbānic cessation citta also has as object a mental or material phenomenon. This (they say) is the same as with the dying javanas, and excludes kamma, the sign of kamma and the sign of destiny. However, this idea is contrary to the general rule of Abhidhamma, which is that, in the same existence, the rebirth citta, the bhavanga citta and the decease citta must have the same object[23].

The Object of Buddha's Decease Citta

Some teachers have said that the object of Buddha's decease citta was Nibbāna. In support of this they cite a passage from the Parinibbāna Sutta: "Anejo santimārabbha, yaṁ kālamakarī muni[24]." The translation of this being: "the Buddha who is free from lust for the sake of Nibbāna, thus awaits the time of Parinibbāna." However, these teachers do not give attention to the Parittārammana-tika in the Dhammasangani. This explains that the 23 sense-sphere resultant cittas, the five-door adverting citta and the smiling citta always have sensuous objects. The Abhidhamma teaching makes no exceptions. The Buddha's parinibbāna decease citta is the same as his birth citta, i.e. the first citta of the eight great resultant sense-sphere cittas. This sensuous resultant citta cannot take Nibbāna as its object. When the Buddha took rebirth into the human world, the object of his rebirth citta was the sign of destiny of the human world. Therefore, the object of parinibbānic decease citta must also be the same sign of destiny. The decease citta (i.e. the final citta in a life term) apprehends the same object that was taken by the rebirth citta and bhavanga citta of the existence that is about to end.

Furthermore, the passage from the Mahāparinibbāna sutta means that being about to enter into parinibbāna, the Buddha was looking for nibbāna. Therefore, the commentary to that sutta did not say "santiṁ ārammanaṁ katvā", meaning "Nibbāna having been made an object". Instead it says "santimarabbhāti anupādisesaṁ nibbānaṁ ārabbha (for the sake of) paṭicca (depends upon) sandhāya (concerning)", meaning "looking for nibbāna without residue remaining". Anupādisesa nibbāna (meaning nibbāna without residue remaining)[25] is experienced by Arahants and Buddhas after death. However, the Theragāthā commentary[26] says "santimarabbhāti santiṁ anupādisesaṁ nibbānaṁ ārammaṇaṁ katvā", meaning "had been the object of the nibbāna without residue remaining". This seems contrary to the commentary of Mahāparinibbāna sutta. However, if it means that prior to the parinibbānic decease process the Buddha had been living with the object of nibbāna and then there is no disagreement between the two commentaries. Of course, prior to the parinibbānic decease citta, the Buddha enters into the jhānic attainments, reviews the jhānic factors and then ceases immediately. In this case, prior to the parinibbānic decease, the kasiṇa concepts appear in his mind. These are the objects of the jhānic attainments. Also the jhānic factors, which are the object of the reviewing process, appear in him. At the end the parinibbānic decease citta arise and cease forever. There is no moment, no instant during which the nibbāna object arises

Thus, one must understand that, prior to the attainment of the jhānic state, the Buddha may or may not live with Nibbāna. However, by looking forward to the Nibbānic state, not at the moment of decease, Nibbāna is not the object of the Parinibbānic decease citta. Instead, the object is the sign of destiny of this last life in Saṁsāra, which was the object of rebirth citta.

Jhāna Immediacy Process

The jhāna immediacy process occurs in the sensuous blissful plane, the fine-material plane and the immaterial plane where jhāna arises as many times as necessary. This process occurs only in arahants, so that the functional cittas function as javanas. The object is a kasiṇa, a concept etc. according to the respective jhānas. The object of the preceding bhavanga and cessation cittas are as usual, one of kamma, sign of kamma or sign of destiny. It is possible that the cessation citta occurs after jhāna or after jhāna and bhavanga. These two types of process multiplied by nine functional cittas, gives eighteen processes (9x2=18) and multiplied by two individuals (keen-witted and dull-witted) becomes thirty-six (18X2=36) processes in total.

Reviewing Immediacy Process

The javanas in this process are sensuous and they arise for five moments only, due to the dying process. They are also found (as jhāna immediacy processes) in the sense-sphere, fine-material and immaterial planes. Their objects are jhānic factors. It is possible that, in the process, cessation arises after javana and bhavanga. Therefore, there are two types of process: in one type cessation arises after javana and in the other type cessation arises after javana and bhavanga. Two processes multiplied by five jhānic factors in the first jhāna (2X5=10) becomes ten processes; multiplied by four factors in the second jhāna (2X4=8) gives eight processes; by three factors in the third jhāna (2X3=6) yields six processes; multiplied by two factors in the fourth jhāna (2X2=4) and by two factors in the fifth jhāna (2X2=4). Thus, there are in total 32 types of processes in the reviewing immediacy dying process. These processes are explained in the commentary of the Mahāparinibbāna Sutta. This commentary says "bhavangaṁ otinnassa tattheva parinibbānaṁ[27]", which means "having subsided into the bhavanga in that bhavanga moment there occurs that attainment of parinibbāna". Thus, there are processes in which bhavanga and ceasing arises, after jhāna or the reviewing process. Cessation citta and bhavanga are the same, meaning there are processes in which the parinibbānic cessation arises after jhāna and the reviewing javana.

Direct Knowledge Immediacy Process

This kind of process is found in the commentary of Udana. There are various kinds of direct knowledge or super-normal powers, but, in this context, direct knowledge (abhiññā) means only Iddhividha abhiññā: the power of creating forms, flying through the air, walking on water, diving into the earth and so on. In the process of the parinibbāna cessation, two types of process arise after abhiññā or after abhiññā and bhavanga. These processes are only found in the sense-sphere plane and fine-material plane. This process cannot occur in the immaterial realm because there is no other jhānic attainment necessary for the direct knowledge process.

Jīvitasamasīsī Process

Ignorance is the head of the defilements and the life-faculty is the head of existence. Therefore, ignorance is the chief of all the defilements and life-span is the chief of the round of suffering, or saṁsāra, conditionality. When ignorance ceases, all traces of defilements also cease. In the same way, when the chain of life-span is cut off, all conditionality of saṁsāric suffering also ceases. For example, take a person who is suffering from a severe disease. He disgusted by the conditionality of saṁsāric suffering and so practises meditation seriously. He develops all the stages of insight. Eventually, with the attainment of the arahatta path, he eradicates ignorance. At the same time, suppose his life-span also ceases. In this situation, ignorance (the head of defilements) and the life-faculty (the head of conditionality) have both ceased in the same moment. This kind of person is called jīvita-sama-sīsī.

It should be noted that, although it is said the ceasing of the life-span and of ignorance occur at the same time, this does not mean in the same moment but in the same process. The moment at which ignorance ceases is the moment of attainment of the arahatta path. After the arahatta path citta arises there follows two or three moments of arahatta fruition. There are some interrupting bhavangas then the process of reviewing occurs. Finally, at the end of the reviewing process, the parinibbānic cessation subsides and the life-span ceases. Thus, the ceasing of ignorance and the end of the life-span occur in the same process, not at the same moment. In the same process, ignorance has ceased and also the life-span has ceased. So it is said that cessation of ignorance and of life-span have an equal time. This process of jīvitasamasīsī is explained in the commentary of Anguttara-nikāya[28]. This process occurs in the sense-sphere plane. It is possible that the cessation arises after javana and bhavanga.

Thus, we have briefly explained the process of consciousness in eight sections: (i) five sense-door process; (ii) sensuous-javana mind-door process; (iii) sublime-javana mind-door (jhāna) process; (iv) the path process; (v) the attainment of fruition process; (vi) abhiññā or direct knowledge process; (vii) the attainment of cessation process and (viii) the dying process[29].

The End of Cognitive Process

CHAPTER V

PROCESS OF MATTER

Rūpa-Matter

Rūpa (matter) is one of the four realities in the Abhidhamma. The word rūpa is generally translated as matter, corporeality, materiality, body, form etc. However, none of these convey the exact meaning of the word, and of them matter is the nearest equivalent. The Pāli word rūpa is explained in the Abhidhamma by pointing to its derivation from the verb "ruppati", which means to be changed or deformed. From a Buddhist standpoint rūpa is not only changed, but also perishes, since it lasts only seventeen mind moments. According to the Vibhāvanīṭīkā[1], rūpa or matter is so called because it both undergoes and imposes alteration, owing to adverse physical conditions such as cold and heat etc. Of course, rūpa may change state, form and colour on account of heat and cold just as matter does. However, although form, shape and mass become apparent when a significant quantity of rūpa has accumulated, in the ultimate sense rūpa is formless, shapeless and without mass, just as energy is.

Scientists now know that matter and energy are equivalent or we might say inter-convertible; in the ultimate sense matter and energy are identical. At the time of the Buddha, an early version of what we now know as atomic theory was prevalent in India. The Indian thinkers spoke of the paramāṇu or atom and they analysed it thus: one rathareṇu consists of 36 tajjāris; one tajjāri is 36 aṇus and one aṇu is 36 paramāṇus. The minute particles of dust seen dancing in a sunbeam are called rathareṇu. One paramāṇu is 1/46,656th part of a rathareṇu. This paramāṇu was considered indivisible. The Buddha analysed matter as the kalāpa, a unity of elements or sub-atomic particles: an ultimate entity, which cannot be further subdivided.

The Abhidhamma enumerates twenty-eight types of material phenomena. These are basically divided into two categories: the four great essentials (mahābhūta) and twenty-four derivative material phenomena (upādārūpa). The four great essentials are the primary material elements (dhātu) of earth, water, fire and air. These are fundamental constituents of matter. They are inseparable and, in their various combinations, enter into the composition of all material substances, from the minutest particle to the massive mountains. Derivative material phenomena are material phenomena rooted in or dependent upon the four great essentials. The great essentials may be compared to the earth, the derivative phenomena to trees and shrubs that grow dependent on the earth.

The twenty-eight types of matter are classified into eleven material qualities:

1. Four essential material qualities: earth element, water element, fire element and air element.(4)
2. Sensitive material qualities: located in the eye, ear, nose, tongue and body.(5)
3. Material qualities of sense objects: visible form, sound, odour and taste[2].(4)
4. Material qualities of sex: femininity and masculinity. (2)
5. Material quality of base: heart-base. (1)
6. Material quality of life: life faculty. (1)
7. Material quality of nutrition: edible food[3]. (1)
8. Material quality of limitation: the element of space. (1)
9. Material quality of communication: bodily intimation and vocal intimation.(2)
10. Material quality of mutability: material lightness, pliancy and adaptability together with two forms of intimation. (3)
11. Material qualities of characteristics: material productivity, continuity, decay and impermanence[4]. (4)

(Please see *A Comprehensive Manual of Abhidhamma*, Chapter VI for details)

Concretely Produced Matter

The material qualities in groups 1 to 7 above (except for tangibility which consists of earth, fire and air elements) make up eighteen material qualities that are collectively named as the concretely produced matter (nipphanna rūpa). This is because they undergo deformation (which is one of the essential characteristics of matter) and they are caused and conditioned by kamma, citta, utu (temperature) and nutrition. Each of these eighteen types of matter have their innate properties such as hardness for the earth element and heat for the fire element. Therefore, they are also called sabhāva rūpa, matter possessing intrinsic nature. Each of these types of matter also have the innate sign or characteristics of birth (jāti), decay (jaratā) and death (aniccatā). So, they are also described as matter possessing real characteristics (salakkhaṇarūpa). This is because they should be contemplated by insight as having the characteristics of impermanence, un-satisfactoriness and not self; they are also called sammasana rūpa: matter to be comprehended by insight.

Non-Concretely Produced Matter

The ten kinds of matter in classes 8 to 11 are designated as non-concretely produced matter (anipphanna rūpa). This is because they do not arise directly from the four main causes of kamma, citta, temperature or nutrition. Instead they exist as modalities or attributes of concretely produced matter. They are also known as asabhāva: matter which does not have innate properties neither do they have the characteristics of birth, decay and death (alakkhanarūpa); and they should not be contemplated by insight meditation. Truly speaking they are not included among the ultimate realities.

Kalāpa - Unity of Elements

The material qualities do not occur singly but in combinations or groups known as rūpākalāpas; tiny material groups or kalāpas. The basic kalāpa consists of the eight elements: the four great essentials of earth, water, fire and air, and their properties of colour (vaṇṇa), odour (gandha), taste (rasa) and nutritive essence (ojā). These qualities are inseparable[5]. There are altogether twenty-one kalāpas enumerated in the Abhidhamma. All material qualities in a kalāpa arise together and cease together. They all depend on the great essentials that are present in the kalāpa for their arising, i.e. they have a common dependence. They are so thoroughly mixed that they cannot be distinguished, so they all occur together, from their arising to their cessation. That is to say: kalāpas are so small that they are invisible, smaller than an atom and are comparable to electrons, protons and neutrons in size.

Kamma Originated Kalāpas[6] (9)

All material phenomena originate from four different causes: kamma, consciousness, temperature or nutriment. Eighteen of the types of material phenomena originate from kamma and they are grouped as nine kalāpas originating from kamma. For example, the physical life-force (which is contained in all kalāpas) and the eight inseparable types of matter, together form the simplest unit of a kamma-born kalāpa. This is called jīvita-navaka-kalāpa, meaning the group of nine types of matter including the life-force. It may be shortened to "vital-nonad".

The nine types of matter may be enumerated as follows:

(1) By adding the basic vital nonad unit to the eye, it is called cakkhudasaka, the eye-decad: consisting of the eight types of inseparable matter, the life faculty and the eye sensitivity;

(2) with the ear, it is called sotadasaka, the ear-decad: consisting of the eight types of inseparable matter, the life faculty and the ear sensitivity;

(3) with the nose, it is called ghāṇadasaka, the nose-decad: consisting of the eight types of inseparable matter, the life faculty and the nose sensitivity;

(4) with the tongue, it is called jīvhādasaka, the tongue-decad: consisting of the eight inseparable types of matter, the life faculty and the tongue sensitivity;

(5) with the body, it is called kāyadasaka, the body-decad: consisting of the eight inseparable types of matter, the life faculty and the body sensitivity;

(6) with the material quality of femininity, it is called

itthibhāvadasaka, the female-decad: consisting of the eight inseparable types of matter, the life faculty and femininity;

(7) with the material quality of masculinity, it is called pumbhāvadasaka, the male-decad: consisting of the eight types of the inseparable matter, the life faculty and masculinity;

(8) with the heart-base, it is called hadayadasaka, the heart-decad: consisting of the eight types of inseparable matter, the life faculty and the heart base; and

(9) jīvita-navaka, the vital-nonad: consisting of the eight types of inseparable matter and the life faculty.

Consciousness Originated Kalāpas[7] (6)

Fourteen types of material phenomena (excluding the limiting phenomenon, i.e. the space element), are grouped as six kalāpas, originating from consciousness.

These may be enumerated as follows:

(1) The original eight types of inseparable matter produced by consciousness are called cittaja-suddhatthaka, the consciousness-born pure-octad: consisting of the eight types of inseparable matter;

(2) by adding the bodily intimation it is called kāyaviññatti-navaka, the bodily intimation-nonad: consisting of the eight types of inseparable matter and the bodily intimation;

(3) with the vocal intimation and sound, it is called vacīviññatti-sadda-navaka, the vocal intimation decad: consisting of the eight types of inseparable matter, the vocal intimation and sound;

(4) with the material qualities of lightness, pliancy and adaptability, it is called lahutādi ekādasaka, the undecad of mutability: consisting of the eight types of inseparable matter and the material qualities of lightness, pliancy and adaptability;

(5) with the bodily intimation and the material qualities of lightness, pliancy and adaptability, it is called kāyaviññatti-lahutādi dvādasaka, the dodecad of mutability: consisting of the eight types of inseparable matter, the bodily intimation and the material

qualities of lightness, pliancy and adaptability; and

(6) with the vocal intimation and sound, the material qualities of lightness, pliancy and adaptability, it is called vacīviññatti-sadda-lahutādi-terasaka, the tri-decad of mutability: consisting of the eight types of inseparable matter, vocal intimation, sound and the material qualities of lightness, pliancy and adaptability.

Temperature Originated Kalāpas[8] (4)

Twelve material phenomena (excluding the limiting phenomenon, i.e. the space element), are grouped as the four kalāpas originating from temperature.

These may be enumerated as follows:

(1) The original eight types of inseparable matter produced by temperature are called utuja-suddhatthaka, temperature-born pure-octad: consisting of the eight types of inseparable matter;

(2) by adding sound, it is called saddanavaka, the sound-nonad: consisting of the eight types of inseparable matter and sound;

(3) with the material qualities of lightness, pliancy and adaptability, it is called lahutādi ekādasaka, the undecad of mutability: consisting of the eight types of inseparable matter and the material qualities of lightness, pliancy and adaptability; and

(4) with sound and the material qualities of lightness, pliancy and adaptability, it is called saddalahutādi dvādasaka, the dodecad of sound and mutability: consisting of the eight types of inseparable matter, sound and the material qualities of lightness, pliancy and adaptability.

Nutriment Originated Kalāpas (2)

Eleven nutriment-born phenomena (excluding the limiting phenomenon, i.e. the space element) are grouped as two kalāpas originating from nutriment.

These may be enumerated as follows:

(1) The original eight types of inseparable matter produced by nutriment are called āhāraja-suddhatthaka, nutriment-born pure-

octad: consisting of the eight types of inseparable matter; and

(2) by adding three aspects of mutability, it is called lahutādi-ekādasaka, the undecad of mutability: consisting of the eight types of inseparable matter and the material qualities of lightness, pliancy and adaptability.

The Occurrence of the Process of Matter

Iccevaṁ, paṭisandhim upādāya kammasamuṭṭhānā, Dutiyacittam upādāya cittasamuṭṭhānā, Ṭhitikālam upādāya utusamuṭṭhānā, Ojāpharaṇam upādāya āhārajasamuṭṭhānā cā ti catusamuṭṭhāna-rūpākalāpasantati kāmaloke dīpajāla viya nadīsoto viya ca yāvatāyukaṁ abbhocchinnaṁ pavattati[9].

"Thus, the continuity of material groups is produced in four ways, namely: kamma-born from the rising instance of the rebirth-linking citta, consciousness-born from the rising instant of the first bhavanga citta (which arises immediately after the rebirth-linking citta), temperature-born from the present instance of the rebirth-linking citta and nutriment-born from the time of the diffusion of nutritive essence- this flows on in the sense-sphere uninterruptedly until the end of life, like the flame of a lamp or the stream of a river."[10]

Traditionally, the process of matter means the process of the group of kalāpas, which are originated by kamma, consciousness, temperature or nutriment. This process is twofold: the process of kalāpas occurring as an individual being in the sense-sphere and in the fine material realm. Buddhism recognizes four kinds of birth, namely: egg-born beings (andaja), womb-born beings (jalābuja), moisture-born beings (saṁsedaja) and beings having a spontaneous birth (opapātika). However, egg-born beings are also implicitly included in the category of womb-born beings, i.e. in the name of womb-born beings, which is gabbhaseyyaka sattā. Thus, the process of the arising of beings in the sense-sphere is of three types: the process of the womb-born beings, of moisture and of spontaneous birth beings. However, we will explain here only the process of womb-born beings.

One may find many other types of kalāpas in Abhidhamma, such as: kamma conditioned nutriment-born kalāpas, citta conditioned nutriment-born kalāpas, temperature conditioned nutriment-born kalāpas, nutriment conditioned nutriment-born kalāpas and the external temperature conditioned temperature-born kalāpas. However, teachers of the Abhidhamma did not mention their process of arising. Therefore, we will explain here only those kalāpas that have been clarified in *A Comprehensive Manual of Abhidhamma.* Also some types of kalāpas, which are originated by citta, temperature and nutriment (such as the sound nonad, the do-decad of sound and mutability etc.) will not be explained here, as they do not arise at all times in the lives of beings. So, we will explain here the process of the pure octad kalāpas, together with the cognitive sequences of the rebirth process, the eye-door process, the attainment of cessation process and the dying process.

The Process of the Material Kalāpas

Kamma-Born Kalāpas

There are four kinds of material kalāpa processes that arise uninterruptedly in the womb-born beings. They are: the kamma-born, consciousness-born, temperature-born and nutriment-born material groups. Of these, three types of kamma-born kalāpas (the body-decad, sex-decad and base-decad) begin to arise from the instance of the arising of the rebirth citta. This means that these three types of kalāpas arise at all instances, from the very first instance of the rebirth consciousness and at the arising of all subsequent cittas (bhavanga).[11]

Therefore, at the instance of the dissolution of the sixteenth bhavanga citta, after the rebirth citta, there are altogether 153 kalāpas. Of these, 3 kalāpas are at the arising stage, 147 kalāpas[12] are at the presence stage and the other 3 are at the dissolving stage. Prior to the arising of the vital-nonad kalāpa, and other decad kalāpas, there are equal numbers at the three instances of every citta. The life-time of each kalāpa is 17 mind-moments or 51 instances.

Consciousness-Born Kalāpas

The consciousness-born kalāpas begin to come into being at the instance of the arising of the first bhavanga citta, which arises immediately after the rebirth citta. After this they arise at the instance of the arising of subsequent cittas[13]. The kalāpas that arise at the instance of the arising of the first bhavanga citta dissolve at the instance of the dissolution of the mind-door adverting citta, as they complete the 17 mind moments of their life-time. There are 17 consciousness-born kalāpas at the instance of the dissolution of the mind-door adverting citta. Of them, 16 are at the presence stage and one is at the dissolving stage. This number remains prior to the arising of the five sense consciousness, and the consciousness born kalāpas do not arise during the attainment of cessation (nirodha-samāpatti). These kalāpas arise only at the instance of the arising of cittas.

Temperature-Born Kalāpas

The fire element (which is called temperature) exists within the three kamma-born kalāpas that arise together with the rebirth citta. This temperature having enough strength at the instance of its own presence stage, and that of the rebirth citta, is able to produce three types of temperature-born kalāpas. This means that the three temperature-born kalāpas begin to arise at the instance of the presence of the rebirth citta, and also new temperature-born kalāpas arise at the instance of its dissolution. In the same way, they arise and dissolve at every instance. These temperature-born kalāpas have connection with the kamma-born kalāpas, so they are called kamma conditioned temperature-born kalāpas[14].

[Table I]

The fire element (temperature) also exists within the consciousness-born kalāpas, which arise at the instance of the arising of the first bhavanga. They also begin to produce one temperature-born kalāpa from the instance of the presence of the first bhavanga. The temperature within the consciousness-born kalāpas, which arise at the instance of the arising of the second bhavanga, produce the temperature-born kalāpa at the instance of the presence stage of the second bhavanga. Thus, consciousness conditioned temperature-born kalāpas also arise at the instance of the presence stage of subsequent cittas. Therefore, there are 13 kamma conditioned temperature-born kalāpas; and 16 at the instance of the dissolution stage of the first bhavanga; 19 at the instance of the arising stage of the second bhavanga; and 23 at the instance of the presence stage of second bhavanga. (Here the 13 kalāpas and 16 kalāpas are referring to many kinds of group of kalāpas that may arise in the body). The processes that are explained here occur at the time of the rebirth process, in which no external nutriment-born kalāpas arise; hence the nutriment-born kalāpas are omitted from this process.

Vital-Nonad Kalāpas

According to the commentaries, the vital-nonad kalāpa arises in sensuous world beings, as the body-decad, in the whole body after the arising of the rebirth citta and arises at any one of three instances of that citta. For example, to facilitate understanding, suppose it arises at the instance of the arising of a citta. There are then 153 kamma-born kalāpas at the instance of the arising of the citta, together with the vital-nonad the total then becomes 154 kalāpas. At the instance of the presence stage, it becomes 155, and at the instance of dissolution stage, it becomes 156 kalāpas. Since its arising, until the 51st instance, there are 204 kamma-born kalāpas. Of these, 4 kalāpas are at the arising stage, 196 kalāpas[15] are at the presence stage and 4 kalāpas are at the dissolving stage. This number will remain the same until the arising of, for example, the eye-decad kalāpa.

The consciousness-born kalāpas are only 17 in number. When the vital-nonad kalāpa arises (at the instance of its presence) the fire-element or temperature (which is accompanied by the vital-nonad) also produces temperature-born kalāpas. Also, at that instance, 170 temperature-born kalāpas are already present, so there are 171 kalāpas in total. Thus, vital-nonad kalāpas are arising at every instance. In addition at every instance of their presence, the number of kamma

conditioned temperature-born kalāpas increase. However, at the arriving of the 51st instance, the original vital-nonad and temperature-born kalāpas that are connected with it cease. When the original vital-nonad kalāpa has completed its life-time of 17 mind moments, there are 220 temperature-born kalāpas present. Then, at the instance of the arising of citta, one kamma conditioned temperature-born kalāpa (connected with the vital-nonad kalāpas) is added, so that there are now 221 kalāpas. Then the number of temperature-born kalāpas neither increases nor decreases any further. Of these 221 kalāpas, 4 kamma conditioned temperature-born kalāpas are at the arising stage, because consciousness conditioned temperature-born kalāpas dissolve at the instance of the arising of citta, 5 kalāpas are at the dissolving stage and 212 kalāpas are at the presence stage. At the instance of the presence of a citta (since the consciousness conditioned temperature-born kalāpa are always arising) 5 kalāpas are at the arising stage, 4 kalāpas are at the dissolving stage and 212 kalāpas are at the presence stage. At the instance of dissolution of a citta, the citta conditioned temperature-born kalāpas have not arisen and dissolved; therefore 4 kalāpas are at the arising stage, 4 kalāpas are at the dissolving stage and 213 kalāpas are at the presence stage.[16]
[This is presented in detail in table II.]

Nutriment-Born Kalāpas

When the nutriment taken by a pregnant mother is pervading the body of the embryo, the nutritive essence that is contained in the nutriment at the instance of presence, produces the nutriment-born kalāpa. The nutriment-born kalāpa could arise at any one of three instances, i.e. arising, presence or dissolving. However, to facilitate understanding, let us take the example of it arising at the instance of the arising of citta. The nutritive essence, which is contained in the nutriment taken by the mother, produces the nutriment-born kalāpas at every instance because the new nutritive essence is arising at every instance. Therefore, at the instance of arising there is one nutriment-born kalāpas, at the instance of presence there are two kalāpas, at the instance of dissolution there are three kalāpas and so on. When the very first nutriment kalāpa arrives at the 51st instance there are 51 kalāpas and of these, 1 kalāpa is at the arising stage, 1 kalāpa is at the dissolving stage and 49 kalāpas are at the presence stage.

Ojāsankhāto āhāro āhārasamuṭṭhānarūpaṁ
ajjhoharaṇakāle ṭhānapattova samuṭṭhāpeti.[17]

Nutriment, known as nutritive essence, on reaching its stage of presence, produces material phenomena originating from nutriment at the time it is swallowed.

There is no increase or decrease in the number of kamma-born and citta-born kalāpas. However, the temperature-born kalāpa arises at the instance of the presence of the very first nutriment-born kalāpas. Therefore, there are 222 kalāpas in total: 221 kalāpas are present and 1 kalāpa is just arising. Thus, the nutriment conditioned temperature-born kalāpa increase one by one at each instance. By the time the 51st instance occurs, the total number has increased by 51 kalāpas, making 272 kalāpas in total. (One should understand the arising, presence and dissolving stages of kalāpas.) Then, until the eye-decad kalāpas and so on arise, the kamma-born, citta-born, temperature-born and nutriment-born kalāpas are neither increasing nor decreasing in number.[18]
[Table III]

Eye-Decad Kalāpa etc.

The four sets of kamma-born kalāpas (i.e. the eye-decad, ear-decad, nose-decad and tongue-decad, according to the commentaries) begin to arise spontaneously in the eleventh week after conception. Although, in reality, there is no way for them to arise at the same time. However, to facilitate understanding, suppose they spontaneously arise at the instance of the arising of a citta. One should understand that if the number of kamma-born kalāpa is increased, then the kamma conditioned temperature-born kalāpa is also increased at the instance of the presence stage. Therefore, when these kalāpas arise at the very first instance of the arising of the citta, there are 204 kamma-born

kalāpas already in existence. By adding 4 new kalāpas the total becomes 208, with 272 temperature-born kalāpas also already existing. At the instance of presence there are 212 kamma-born kalāpas and 276 temperature-born kalāpas. At the instance of dissolution there are 216 kamma-born kalāpas and 280 temperature-born kalāpas in existence. Thus, until the arriving of the 51st instance, the number of kalāpas increases by 4 at each instance. At the 51st instance there are 408 kamma-born kalāpas; and at the next instance 476 temperature born kalāpas present. (One should understand the arising, presence and dissolving stages of kalāpas.) These kalāpas remain the same in number at all times, except for the time of the five-door cognitive process and the attainment of cessation process.[19]
[Table IV]

Five-Door Cognitive Process

The series of material kalāpas arises during the five-door cognitive process. The five types of sense consciousness cannot produce matter so, at the instance of their arising, there are only 16 citta-born kalāpas. Of these, 15 kalāpas are at the presence stage and 1 is at the dissolving stage. This means that from the very first instance of the arising of the series of sense consciousness, till the 51st instance of dissolution (i.e. the 17th mind moment), there are only 16 citta-born kalāpas. At the dissolution instance of the 17th mind moment there are none at the dissolving stage but all 16 kalāpas are at the presence stage. However, at the instance of the arising of the 18th mind moment one citta-born kalāpa arises and the total number then becomes 17 kalāpas. Thereafter, the number is neither increased nor decreased.[20]
[Table V]

The Attainment of Cessation

There is no consciousness during the attainment of cessation. Therefore, at the dissolution instance of the neither perception nor non-perception javana stage only 17 citta-born kalāpas are in existence. Then, with every three instances one kalāpa ceases so, at

the moment of the 16th citta all citta-born kalāpas have ceased. When emerging from the attainment of cessation, at the instance of the arising of either the non-returner javana or the arahanta javana, the citta-born kalāpas arise one by one at each instance. At the 17th mind-moment, 17 citta-born kalāpas are present as usual. Temperature-born kalāpas are increased or decreased, according to the increase or decrease of the citta-born kalāpas. However, the number of kamma-born kalāpas remains the same without change, until the dying moment.[21]
[Table VI &VII]

Dying Moment

There are twenty-one material groups called kalāpas: nine, six, four, and two produced by kamma, citta, temperature and nutriment respectively; which flow on until the end of life, as the stream of a river or the flame of a lamp. This is what we call the human body. In other words, the human body is made up of tiny kalāpas that are arising and passing away every moment, billions of times during a single lifetime. Most of them cease from their process of arising and passing away at the time of death. How does this occur?

At the time of death the kamma-born kalāpas no longer arise, starting from the instance of the presence of the seventeenth consciousness (citta) preceding the death consciousness. Their number is reduced from one instance to another, and at the instance of the dissolution stage of the death consciousness, all kamma-born kalāpas have ceased for ever in this present life.

Neither do the consciousness-born kalāpas arise after the death consciousness. From their cessation the number of the consciousness-born kalāpas is reduced one by one, at every instance. At the 48th instance, after the death consciousness, all the consciousness-born kalāpas have ceased their existence.

The nutriment-born kalāpas can arise until the instance of the dissolving of the death consciousness. Therefore, they have ceased totally only at the 50th instance after the death consciousness.

However, the temperature-born kalāpas persist in the form of the corpse and, thereafter, remain as a process of rising and vanishing with different forms accordingly.[22]
[Table VIII]

Table 1: Process of Kalāpas at the Time of Conception

Citta	Instance	Kamma born	Citta born	Temperature born	Total Kalāpas
Rebirth Citta	Arising	3	x	x	3
	Presence	6	x	3	9
	Dissolution	9	x	6	15
1 Bhavanga	Arising	12	1	9	22
	Presence	15	1	13	29
	Dissolution	18	1	16	35
2 Bhavanga	Arising	21	2	19	42
	Presence	24	2	23	49
	Dissolution	27	2	26	55
3 Bhavanga	Arising	30	3	29	62
	Presence	33	3	33	69
	Dissolution	36	3	36	75
4 Bhavanga	Arising	39	4	39	82
	Presence	42	4	43	89
	Dissolution	45	4	46	95
5 Bhavanga	Arising	48	5	49	102
	Presence	51	5	53	109
	Dissolution	54	5	56	115
6 Bhavanga	Arising	57	6	59	122
	Presence	60	6	63	129
	Dissolution	63	6	66	135
7 Bhavanga	Arising	66	7	69	142
	Presence	69	7	73	149
	Dissolution	72	7	76	155
8 Bhavanga	Arising	75	8	79	162
	Presence	78	8	83	169
	Dissolution	81	8	86	175
9 Bhavanga	Arising	84	9	89	182
	Presence	87	9	93	189
	Dissolution	90	9	96	195
10 Bhavanga	Arising	93	10	99	202
	Presence	96	10	103	209
	Dissolution	99	10	106	215
11 Bhavanga	Arising	102	11	109	222
	Presence	105	11	113	229
	Dissolution	108	11	116	235

12 Bhavanga	Arising	111	12	119	242
	Presence	114	12	123	249
	Dissolution	117	12	126	255
13 Bhavanga	Arising	120	13	129	262
	Presence	123	13	133	269
	Dissolution	126	13	136	275
14 Bhavanga	Arising	129	14	139	282
	Presence	132	14	143	289
	Dissolution	135	14	146	295
15 Bhavanga	Arising	138	15	149	302
	Presence	141	15	153	309
	Dissolution	144	15	156	315
16 Bhavanga	Arising	147	16	159	322
	Presence	150	16	163	329
	Dissolution	153	16	166	335
17 Bhavanga	Arising	153	17	169	339
	Presence	153	17	170	340
	Dissolution	153	17	170	340
18 Bhavanga	Arising	153	17	170	340
	Presence	153	17	170	340
	Dissolution	153	17	170	340

Table 2: Process of Kalāpas at the Time of Arising of the Vital (life) Nonad Kalāpas

Citta	Instance	Kamma born	Citta born	Temperature born	Total Kalāpas
Citta	Arising	154	17	170	341
	Presence	155	17	171	343
	Dissolution	156	17	172	345
Citta	Arising	157	17	173	347
	Presence	158	17	174	349
	Dissolution	159	17	175	351
Citta	Arising	160	17	176	353
	Presence	161	17	177	355
	Dissolution	162	17	178	357
Citta	Arising	163	17	179	359
	Presence	164	17	180	361
	Dissolution	165	17	181	363
Citta	Arising	166	17	182	365
	Presence	167	17	183	367
	Dissolution	168	17	184	369
Citta	Arising	169	17	185	371
	Presence	170	17	186	373
	Dissolution	171	17	187	375
Citta	Arising	172	17	188	377
	Presence	173	17	189	379
	Dissolution	174	17	190	381
Citta	Arising	175	17	191	383
	Presence	176	17	192	385
	Dissolution	177	17	193	387
Citta	Arising	178	17	194	389
	Presence	179	17	195	391
	Dissolution	180	17	196	393
Citta	Arising	181	17	197	395
	Presence	182	17	198	397
	Dissolution	183	17	199	399
Citta	Arising	184	17	200	401
	Presence	185	17	201	403
	Dissolution	186	17	202	405
Citta	Arising	187	17	203	407
	Presence	188	17	204	409
	Dissolution	189	17	205	411

Citta	Arising	190	17	206	413
	Presence	191	17	207	415
	Dissolution	192	17	208	417
Citta	Arising	193	17	209	419
	Presence	194	17	210	421
	Dissolution	195	17	211	423
Citta	Arising	196	17	212	425
	Presence	197	17	213	427
	Dissolution	198	17	214	429
Citta	Arising	199	17	215	431
	Presence	200	17	216	433
	Dissolution	201	17	217	435
Citta	Arising	202	17	218	437
	Presence	203	17	219	439
	Dissolution	204	17	220	441
Citta	Arising	204	17	221	442
	Presence	204	17	221	442
	Dissolution	204	17	221	442

Table 3: Process of Kalāpas at the Time of Arising of the Nutriment-Born Kalāpas

Citta	Instance	Kamma born	Citta born	Nutriment born	Temperature born	Total Kalāpas
Citta	Arising	204	17	1	221	443
	Presence	204	17	2	222	445
	Dissolution	204	17	3	223	447
Citta	Arising	204	17	4	224	449
	Presence	204	17	5	225	451
	Dissolution	204	17	6	226	453
Citta	Arising	204	17	7	227	455
	Presence	204	17	8	228	457
	Dissolution	204	17	9	229	459
Citta	Arising	204	17	10	230	461
	Presence	204	17	11	231	463
	Dissolution	204	17	12	232	465
Citta	Arising	204	17	13	233	467
	Presence	204	17	14	234	469
	Dissolution	204	17	15	235	471
Citta	Arising	204	17	16	236	473
	Presence	204	17	17	237	475
	Dissolution	204	17	18	238	477
Citta	Arising	204	17	19	239	479
	Presence	204	17	20	240	481
	Dissolution	204	17	21	241	483
Citta	Arising	204	17	22	242	485
	Presence	204	17	23	243	487
	Dissolution	204	17	24	244	489
Citta	Arising	204	17	25	245	491
	Presence	204	17	26	246	493
	Dissolution	204	17	27	247	495
Citta	Arising	204	17	28	248	497
	Presence	204	17	29	249	499
	Dissolution	204	17	30	250	501
Citta	Arising	204	17	31	251	503
	Presence	204	17	32	252	505
	Dissolution	204	17	33	253	507
Citta	Arising	204	17	34	254	509
	Presence	204	17	35	255	511
	Dissolution	204	17	36	256	513

Citta	Arising	204	17	37	257	515
	Presence	204	17	38	258	517
	Dissolution	204	17	39	259	519
Citta	Arising	204	17	40	260	521
	Presence	204	17	41	261	523
	Dissolution	204	17	42	262	525
Citta	Arising	204	17	43	263	527
	Presence	204	17	44	264	529
	Dissolution	204	17	45	265	531
Citta	Arising	204	17	46	266	533
	Presence	204	17	47	267	535
	Dissolution	204	17	48	268	537
Citta	Arising	204	17	49	269	539
	Presence	204	17	50	270	541
	Dissolution	204	17	51	271	543
Citta	Arising	204	17	51	272	544
	Presence	204	17	51	272	544
	Dissolution	204	17	51	272	544

Table 4: Process of Kalāpas at the Time of Arising of the Eye Decad etc.

Citta	Instance	Kamma born	Citta born	Nutriment born	Temperature born	Total Kalāpas
Citta	Arising	208	17	51	272	548
	Presence	212	17	51	276	556
	Dissolution	216	17	51	280	564
Citta	Arising	220	17	51	284	572
	Presence	224	17	51	288	580
	Dissolution	228	17	51	292	588
Citta	Arising	232	17	51	296	596
	Presence	236	17	51	300	604
	Dissolution	240	17	51	304	612
Citta	Arising	244	17	51	308	620
	Presence	248	17	51	312	628
	Dissolution	252	17	51	316	636
Citta	Arising	256	17	51	320	644
	Presence	260	17	51	324	652
	Dissolution	264	17	51	328	660
Citta	Arising	268	17	51	332	668
	Presence	272	17	51	336	676
	Dissolution	276	17	51	340	684
Citta	Arising	280	17	51	344	692
	Presence	284	17	51	348	700
	Dissolution	288	17	51	352	708
Citta	Arising	292	17	51	356	716
	Presence	296	17	51	360	724
	Dissolution	300	17	51	364	732
Citta	Arising	304	17	51	368	740
	Presence	308	17	51	372	748
	Dissolution	312	17	51	376	756
Citta	Arising	316	17	51	380	764
	Presence	320	17	51	384	772
	Dissolution	324	17	51	388	780
Citta	Arising	328	17	51	392	788
	Presence	332	17	51	396	796
	Dissolution	336	17	51	400	804
Citta	Arising	340	17	51	404	812
	Presence	344	17	51	408	820
	Dissolution	348	17	51	412	828

Citta	Arising	352	17	51	416	836
	Presence	356	17	51	420	844
	Dissolution	360	17	51	424	852
Citta	Arising	364	17	51	428	860
	Presence	368	17	51	432	868
	Dissolution	372	17	51	436	876
Citta	Arising	376	17	51	440	884
	Presence	380	17	51	444	892
	Dissolution	384	17	51	448	900
Citta	Arising	388	17	51	452	908
	Presence	392	17	51	456	916
	Dissolution	396	17	51	460	924
Citta	Arising	400	17	51	464	932
	Presence	404	17	51	468	940
	Dissolution	408	17	51	472	948
Citta	Arising	408	17	51	476	952
	Presence	408	17	51	476	952
	Dissolution	408	17	51	476	952

Table 5: Process of Kalāpas at the Time of Arising of the Five Sense Consciousness

Citta	Instance	Kamma born	Citta born	Nutriment born	Temperature born	Total Kalāpas
Past Bhavanga	Arising	408	17	51	476	952
	Presence	408	17	51	476	952
	Dissolution	408	17	51	476	952
Vibrating Bhavanga	Arising	408	17	51	476	952
	Presence	408	17	51	476	952
	Dissolution	408	17	51	476	952
Arresting Bhavanga	Arising	408	17	51	476	952
	Presence	408	17	51	476	952
	Dissolution	408	17	51	476	952
Five-door Adverting	Arising	408	17	51	476	952
	Presence	408	17	51	476	952
	Dissolution	408	17	51	476	952
Sense-consciousness	Arising	408	16	51	475	950
	Presence	408	16	51	475	950
	Dissolution	408	16	51	475	950
Receiving	Arising	408	16	51	475	950
	Presence	408	16	51	475	950
	Dissolution	408	16	51	475	950
Investigating	Arising	408	16	51	475	950
	Presence	408	16	51	475	950
	Dissolution	408	16	51	475	950
Determining	Arising	408	16	51	475	950
	Presence	408	16	51	475	950
	Dissolution	408	16	51	475	950
Javana	Arising	408	16	51	475	950
	Presence	408	16	51	475	950
	Dissolution	408	16	51	475	950
Javana	Arising	408	16	51	475	950
	Presence	408	16	51	475	950
	Dissolution	408	16	51	475	950
Javana	Arising	408	16	51	475	950
	Presence	408	16	51	475	950
	Dissolution	408	16	51	475	950
Javana	Arising	408	16	51	475	950
	Presence	408	16	51	475	950
	Dissolution	408	16	51	475	950

Javana	Arising	408	16	51	475	950
	Presence	408	16	51	475	950
	Dissolution	408	16	51	475	950
Javana	Arising	408	16	51	475	950
	Presence	408	16	51	475	950
	Dissolution	408	16	51	475	950
Javana	Arising	408	16	51	475	950
	Presence	408	16	51	475	950
	Dissolution	408	16	51	475	950
Registering	Arising	408	16	51	475	950
	Presence	408	16	51	475	950
	Dissolution	408	16	51	475	950
Registering	Arising	408	16	51	475	950
	Presence	408	16	51	475	950
	Dissolution	408	16	51	475	950
Bhavanga	Arising	408	16	51	475	950
	Presence	408	16	51	475	950
	Dissolution	408	16	51	475	950
Bhavanga	Arising	408	16	51	475	950
	Presence	408	16	51	475	950
	Dissolution	408	16	51	475	950
Bhavanga	Arising	408	16	51	475	950
	Presence	408	16	51	475	950
	Dissolution	408	16	51	475	950
Bhavanga	Arising	408	16	51	475	950
	Presence	408	16	51	475	950
	Dissolution	408	16	51	475	950
Bhavanga	Arising	408	17	51	475	951
	Presence	408	17	51	476	952
	Dissolution	408	17	51	476	952

Table 6: Process of Kalāpas at the Attainment of Cessation

Citta	Instance	Kamma born	Citta born	Nutriment born	Temperature born	Total Kalāpas
Jhāna	Arising	408	17	51	476	952
	Presence	408	17	51	476	952
	Dissolution	408	17	51	476	952
Jhāna	Arising	408	17	51	476	952
	Presence	408	17	51	476	952
	Dissolution	408	17	51	476	952
From this instance the process of consciousness is ceased.		408	16	51	476	951
		408	16	51	475	950
		408	16	51	475	950
		408	15	51	474	949
		408	15	51	474	948
		408	15	51	474	948
		408	14	51	474	947
		408	14	51	473	946
		408	14	51	473	946
		408	13	51	473	945
		408	13	51	472	944
		408	13	51	472	944
		408	12	51	472	943
		408	12	51	471	942
		408	12	51	471	942
		408	11	51	471	941
		408	11	51	470	940
		408	11	51	470	940
		408	10	51	470	939
		408	10	51	469	938
		408	10	51	469	938
		408	9	51	469	937
		408	9	51	468	936
		408	9	51	468	936
		408	8	51	468	935
		408	8	51	467	934
		408	8	51	467	934
		408	7	51	467	933
		408	7	51	466	932
		408	7	51	466	932

		408	6	51	466	931
		408	6	51	465	930
		408	6	51	465	930
		408	5	51	465	929
		408	5	51	464	928
		408	5	51	464	928
		408	4	51	464	927
		408	4	51	463	926
		408	4	51	463	926
		408	3	51	463	925
		408	3	51	462	924
		408	3	51	462	924
		408	2	51	462	923
		408	2	51	461	922
		408	2	51	461	922
		408	1	51	461	921
		408	1	51	460	920
		408	1	51	460	920
		408		51	460	919
		408		51	459	918
		408		51	459	918

Table 7: Process of Kalāpas at the Time of Emerging from Cessation

Citta	Instance	Kamma born	Citta born	Nutriment born	Temperature born	Total Kalāpas
Fruition	Arising	408	1	51	459	919
	Presence	408	1	51	460	920
	Dissolution	408	1	51	460	920
Bhavanga	Arising	408	2	51	460	921
	Presence	408	2	51	461	922
	Dissolution	408	2	51	461	922
Bhavanga	Arising	408	3	51	461	923
	Presence	408	3	51	462	924
	Dissolution	408	3	51	462	924
Bhavanga	Arising	408	4	51	462	925
	Presence	408	4	51	463	926
	Dissolution	408	4	51	463	926
Bhavanga	Arising	408	5	51	463	927
	Presence	408	5	51	464	928
	Dissolution	408	5	51	464	928
Bhavanga	Arising	408	6	51	464	929
	Presence	408	6	51	465	930
	Dissolution	408	6	51	465	930
Bhavanga	Arising	408	7	51	465	931
	Presence	408	7	51	466	932
	Dissolution	408	7	51	466	932
Bhavanga	Arising	408	8	51	466	933
	Presence	408	8	51	467	934
	Dissolution	408	8	51	467	934
Bhavanga	Arising	408	9	51	467	935
	Presence	408	9	51	468	936
	Dissolution	408	9	51	468	936
Bhavanga	Arising	408	10	51	468	937
	Presence	408	10	51	469	938
	Dissolution	408	10	51	469	938
Bhavanga	Arising	408	11	51	469	939
	Presence	408	11	51	470	940
	Dissolution	408	11	51	470	940
Bhavanga	Arising	408	12	51	470	941
	Presence	408	12	51	471	942
	Dissolution	408	12	51	471	942

Bhavanga	Arising	408	13	51	471	943
	Presence	408	13	51	472	944
	Dissolution	408	13	51	472	944
Bhavanga	Arising	408	14	51	472	945
	Presence	408	14	51	473	946
	Dissolution	408	14	51	473	946
Bhavanga	Arising	408	15	51	473	947
	Presence	408	15	51	474	948
	Dissolution	408	15	51	474	948
Bhavanga	Arising	408	16	51	474	949
	Presence	408	16	51	475	950
	Dissolution	408	16	51	475	950
Bhavanga	Arising	408	17	51	475	951
	Presence	408	17	51	476	952
	Dissolution	408	17	51	476	952

Table 8: Process of Kalāpas at the Time of Dying

Citta	Instance	Kamma born	Citta born	Nutriment born	Temperature born	Total Kalāpas
Past Bhavanga	Arising	408	17	51	476	952
	Presence	400	17	51	476	944
	Dissolution	392	17	51	468	928
Vibrating Bhavanga	Arising	384	17	51	460	912
	Presence	376	17	51	452	896
	Dissolution	368	17	51	444	880
Arresting Bhavanga	Arising	360	17	51	436	864
	Presence	352	17	51	428	848
	Dissolution	344	17	51	420	832
Five-door Adverting	Arising	336	17	51	412	816
	Presence	328	17	51	404	800
	Dissolution	320	17	51	396	784
Eye-consciousness	Arising	312	16	51	388	767
	Presence	304	16	51	379	751
	Dissolution	296	16	51	371	734
Receiving	Arising	288	16	51	363	718
	Presence	280	16	51	355	702
	Dissolution	272	16	51	347	686
Investigating	Arising	264	16	51	339	670
	Presence	256	16	51	331	654
	Dissolution	248	16	51	323	638
Determining	Arising	240	16	51	315	622
	Presence	232	16	51	307	606
	Dissolution	224	16	51	299	590
Javana	Arising	216	16	51	291	574
	Presence	208	16	51	283	558
	Dissolution	200	16	51	275	542
Javana	Arising	192	16	51	267	526
	Presence	184	16	51	259	510
	Dissolution	176	16	51	251	484
Javana	Arising	168	16	51	243	478
	Presence	160	16	51	235	462
	Dissolution	152	16	51	227	446
Javana	Arising	144	16	51	219	430
	Presence	136	16	51	211	414
	Dissolution	128	16	51	203	398

Javana	Arising	120	16	51	195	385
	Presence	112	16	51	187	366
	Dissolution	104	16	51	179	350
Registering	Arising	96	16	51	171	334
	Presence	88	16	51	163	318
	Dissolution	80	16	51	155	302
Registering	Arising	72	16	51	147	286
	Presence	64	16	51	139	270
	Dissolution	56	16	51	131	254
Bhavanga	Arising	48	16	51	123	238
	Presence	40	16	51	115	222
	Dissolution	32	16	51	107	206
Death	Arising	24	16	51	99	190
	Presence	16	16	51	91	174
	Dissolution	8	16	51	83	158

NOTES

INTRODUCTION

1. (Ekaccharakkhaṇe koṭisatasahassasankhyā uppajjitvā nirujjhanti) Smv. P. 31 (Accharasanghātakkhaṇe anekakoṭi satasahassa sankhā vedanā uppajjhanti ti hi aṭṭhakathāyaṁ vuttaṁ) PD, p. 148
2. Dhp. Vers.I
3. AS See (Ch.I&IV)
4. PCM See (Pañcadvāra vīthi)
5. PCM See (manodvāra vīthi)
6. PCM See (Ch.III)
7. PCM See (Ch.III, dying process)
8. PCM See (Ch.IV)
9. PCM See (ChVI, p.246)

CHAPTER I

1. Asl. p. 3
2. CMA p. 25
3. CMA p. 28
4. CMA p. 77
5. CMA p. 83
6. CMA p. 85
7. CMA p. 88
8. CMA p. 89
9. CMA p. 90
10. CMA p. 119
11. CMA p. 122
12. CMA p. 129
13. CMA p. 135
14. CMA p. 144

CHAPTER II

1. Vibhv. 105
2. 17x3 = 51- 2 = 49 moments

3. PD 122 See Vibhv. 105
4. Smv. 34 See PD 123
5. Vibhv. 106 See PD 126
6. CMA 153
7. In the Abhidhamma the word "taste" in this context includes sensations from any of the five sense doors.
8. Vh. 109 See Smv. 219
9. In the Abhidhamma the term" sensual beings" is used to refer to humans and celestial beings (devas)
10. CMA 175
11. CMA 174
12. Heretic = One who has never had contacted with the Buddha's teachings.
13. CMA 153
14. Vism. 7
15. CMA 159
16. Vism. 9
17. 2 upekkhāsantīraṇa citta
    8 Mahāvipāka citta
    5 Rūpāvacara citta
    4 Arūpāvacara citta (See CMA, III, p.122)
18. 50-2 = 48

CHAPTER III

1. Bhavangacalana
2. Tadanuvattika manodvāra vīthi or Anubandhika vīthi
3. Anipphanna rūpa means matters which do not possess intrinsic nature.
4. CMA, P240
5. Nipphanna rūpa means matters which possess intrinsic nature.
6. Smv. 391 (Nyā ṇavibhaṅga Aṭṭhakathā)
7. CMA 175
8. CMA 171
9. Kāyaviññattirūpa and Vacīviññattirūpa

10. VhT. (Mulatika-Nyāṇavibhaṅga) ****
11. 1+29+11 = 41
12. PD 165
13. For more detail see CMA Ch. IV
14. Yadi vibhūta-marammaṇaṁ āpāta māgacchati. (CMA 163)
15. vibhūta rammaṇa
16. Avibhūta rammaṇa
17. atīta = past object, gahaṇa = taking, vīthi = process
18. samūha = whole object, gahaa = taking
19. attha = form or shape, gahaṇa = taking
20. nāma = name of an object, gahaṇa = taking
21. Saddatthabhedacint , Verse No. 11
22. PD 164
23. PD 164
24. Hearing the word "come" is just an example

CHAPTER IV

1. Ākāsānancāyatana
2. Viññānancāyatana
3. Ākincaññāyatana
4. Nevasaññā-nāsaññāyatana
5. See detail CMA 72—73
6. Pathāna (7th Abhidhamma) Vol. I, p.138
7. Visuddhimagga Mahātīkā, Vol.II, p.479-480
8. i) Iddhhividha Abhiññā
   ii) Dibbasota Abhiññā
   iii) Paracittavijānana Abhiññā
   iv) Pubbenivāsānussati Abhiññā
   v) Dibbacakkhu Abhiññā
   vi) Yathākammupaga Abhiññā
   vii) Anāgataṁsa Abhiññā
9. i) Adhiṭṭhāniddhi
   ii) Vikubbaniddhi
   iii) Manomayiddhi

10. For more details see the Path of Purification, p.410
11. Op.Cit.
12. Cittaja rūpa
13. parikamma, upacāra, anuloma and gotrabhū
14. Some teachers say that this occurs after one jhāna.
15. PP 824--833
16. Successful kamma
17. Tihetukapaṭisandhi = A linking consciousness associates with alobha, adosa and amoha.
18. See ten kinds of Kasiṇa, CMA, 330
19. Arahanta never come back to any existence including the sense-sphere plane.
20. Asaññasatta
21. Brahmalokagatā heṭṭhā ariya nopapajjare.........
    i) jhānasamanantara vīthi
    ii) Peccavekkhasamanantara vīthi
    iii) Abhiññāsamanantara vīthi
    iv) Jīvitasamasīsī vīthi
22. Vibhv. (120
23. Paṭisandhi bhavanganca, tathācavana manasaṁ. Ekameva tatheveka,visayanceka jātiyaṁ. (See CMA, 199)
24. Di. II, 128 **The literal translation**: anejo = who's free from lust; muni = sage, the Buddha; santiṁ = to Nibbāna; ārabbha = for sake of; kālaṁ = the time of parinibbāna; yaṁ akarī = thus done.
25. DiA.II, 186
26. Theragāthā Atthakathā, p. 389
27. DiA.II, 187)
28. jīvita = life faculty, sama = equality, sīsa = head. Jīvitena samaṁ sisaṁ yassāti jīvitasamasīsī. Whose cessation of the life-faculty has equality as in the cessation of his ignorance.
29. AnA. (Sattaka nipāta)
    i) Pañcadvāra vīthi
    ii) (Kāmajavanavāra) manodvāra vīthi

iii) (Appanājavanavāra) jhāna vīthi
iv) " Magga vīthi
v) " Phala vīthi
vi) " Abhiññā vīthi
vii) " Nirodhasamāpatti vīthi
viii) " Maraṇāsanna vīthi

CHAPTER V

1. Smv.
2. Tangibility is a part of the three elements of earth, fire and air.
3. 4+5+4+2+1+1+1 = 18 are said that Nipphanna rūpa etc.(See CMA)240
4. 1+2+3+4 = 10 are said that Anipphanna rūpa etc. (See CMA 242)
5. CMA 244-246
6. CMA 253
7. CMA 253
8. CMA 253-254
9. CMA 254
10. CMA 256
11. CMA 247
12. 51x3 = 153 - (3+3) = 147
13. CMA 247
14. CMA 250 (table I)
15. 51x4 = 204 - (4+4) = 196
16. table II
17. CMA 250
18. table III
19. table IV
20. table V
21. table VI & VII
22. table VIII

BIBLIOGRAPHY

Abhidhammatthasanghaha, Ven. Anuruddha, Ministry of Religious Affairs, Yangon, Myanmar, 1957

Abhidhamma Prakasinī (Hindi Commentary of Abhidhammattha Sangaha) 2 Vols, Bhaddanta Rewata Dhamma, Sanskrit University, Varanasi, India, 1967

Abhidhammattha Sangaha with Vibhāvanī Tīka, Edited by Bhaddanta Rewata Dhamma (Pāli in Devanagari Script), Bauddhaswadhyaya Satra, Varanasi, India, 1965

Abhidhammattha Sangaha (Basic Sanghaha), in Myanmar Commentary, by Ashin Janakabhivamsa, Mahagandhayone Pub., Amarapura, Myanmar, 1995

Aṭṭhasālinī, Ven. Buddhaghosa, Ministry of Religious Affairs, Yangon, Myanmar, 1957

A Comprehensive Manual of Abhidhamma, General Editor–Bhikkhu Bodhi, Buddhist Publication Society, Kandy, Sri Lanka, 1999.

The Essence of Buddha Abhidhamma, Dr. Mehm Tin Mon, Radanar Mon Pub., Yangon, Myanmar 1995

A Manual of Abhidhamma, Nārada Mahāthera, Buddhist Publication Society, Kandy, 1980.

The Path of Purification, Ven. Nyānamoli, Buddhist Publication Society, Kandy, Sri Lanka, 1975

Paramatthadīpanī, Ledi Sayadaw, Icchāsaya Press, Yangon, Myanmar, 1956

Sammohavinodinī, Ven. Buddhaghosa, MRA, Yangon, Myanmar,1968

Vibhaṅga Pāli, MRA, Yangon, Myanmar, 2000

Vīthi-Hsoyoe and Myanmar Commentary, by Ashin Janakabhivamsa, New Burma Pitaka Press, Amarapura, Myanmar, 1954

Visuddhimagga, Ven. Buddhaghosa, MRA, Yangon, Myanmar, 1980

PĀLI-ENGLISH GLOSSARY

akusala - unwholesome
akusala cetasikas - unwholesome factors
añña - other
aññanamāna cetasikas - ethically variable factors
aññasamāna - ethically variable (lit. common to the other)
ati-avibhūta - the process of a very obscure object
ati-iṭṭha - the extremely desirable
ati-vibhūta - the process of a very clear object
atiparitta - object termed "very slight"
atīta-bhavanga- past bhavanga
atthaggahaṇa vīthi - the process discerning the substance (form or shape) of the object
adukkha-masukha - neither unpleasant nor pleasant feeling
adosa - non-hatred
addhānaparicchedа - the limit of the life duration
adhimokkha - decision
anāgataṁsa ñāṇa - the power of knowing future existences and future worlds.
aniccatā - death
aniṭṭha - the undesirable
anipphanna rūpa - non-concretely produced matter
anubandhika vīthi - consequent process
anuloma - conformity
anottappa - fearlessness of wrong doing
anga - factor
andaja - egg-born beings birth
appanā-javanavāra - mind-door process (absorption Javana)
appanā javanavāra- manodvāra vīthi - absorption javana in the mind-door process
appamaññā - the illimitables
abhiññā - direct knowledge; higher knowledge or supernormal powers
abhiññā vīthi - direct knowledge process
abhidhamma - the analytic doctrine of the Buddhist Canon
amoha - non-delusion
ariya - a noble one
arūpa - immaterial
arūpāvacara vipāka - immaterial-sphere resultants
alakkhaṇa rūpa - matter without innate properties

alobha - non-greed
āvajjana kicca - the function of adverting
aviparīta - immutable
avibhūta - object is termed "obscure"
asabhāva - matter with innate properties
asura - cowardly or sluggish (person)
ahirika - shamelessness
ahetu - rootless
ahetuka - causeless
ahetuka-kiriya - rootless functionals
āgantuka-bhavanga - the transitional life-continuum (lit. āgantuka: "a visitor")
ātman - soul or atta
ādikammika - the process of beginner
āyatana - (twelve) bases
ālambana - object
āhāraja-suddhatthaka - inseparable matter produced by nutriment

iṭṭha - desirable
iṭṭhamajjhatta – moderately desirable
itthibhāvadasaka - the material quality of femininity
iddhividha abhiññā - the power of creating forms, flying through the air, walking on water, diving into the earth and so on.
indriya - faculties (types of feeling)
issā - envy

uggaha-nimitta - acquired or learning sign
utu - temperature
utuja-suddhatthaka - inseparable matter produced by temperature
uddhacca - restlessness
upacāra - access
upacāra samādhi - neighbourhood concentration
upādārūpa - material phenomena
upekkhā - neutral feeling or equanimity
upekkhā-brahmavihāra - the equanimous sublime state
uppāda - the arising instant or genesis

ekaggatā - one-pointedness of mind
ojā - nutritive essence
ottappa - fear of wrong doing

opapātika - beings having a spontaneous birth

kaṭattā - reserve (kamma); kamma-born matters
kamma - action, deed
kamanimitta - sign of kamma
karuṇā - compassion
kalāpa - group
kasiṇa - meditation device
kāma-javana vīthi - sense-sphere javana process
kāmāvacara vipāka - sense-sphere resultant
kāyadasaka - the body-decad
kāya-dvāra- vīthi - body-door cognitive process
kāyapassaddhi - tranquillity of the mental body
kāyapāguññatā - proficiency of mental body
kāyamudutā - malleability of the mental body
kāyakammaññatā - wieldiness of mental body
kāyalahutā - lightness of the mental body
kāya-vatthu - body-base
kāyaviññatti-lahutādi dvādasaka - the dodecad of mutability
kāyaviññatti-navaka - the bodily intimation-nonad
kāya-viññāṇa - body-consciousness
kāya-viññāṇa-dhātu - body-consciousness element
kāyujukatā - rectitude of mental body
kāraṇa - cause
kicca - function
kiriya - functional
kusala - wholesome
kukkucca - worry
khaṇa - minor instant, moment
gati-nimitta - sign of destiny
gandha - odour
gabbhaseyyaka sattā - womb-born beings
gotrabhū - change-of-lineage
ghāṇadasaka - the nose-decad
ghāṇa-dvāra-vīthi - the nose-door cognitive process
ghāṇa-viññāna - nose-consciousness
ghāṇa-viññāna-dhātu - nose-consciousness element
ghāṇa-vatthu - nose-base

cakkhudasaka - the eye-decad
cakkhu-dvāra-vīthi - the eye-door cognitive process
cakkhu-vatthu - eye-base
cakkhu-viññāna - eye-

consciousness
cakkhu-viññāna-dhātu - eye-consciousness element
citta - consciousness
cittakammaññatā - wieldiness of consciousness
cittakkhaṇa - moment of consciousness
citta-niyāma - fixed order of consciousness, cosmic law of consciousness
cittapāguññatā - proficiency of consciousness
cittapassaddhi - tranquillity of consciousness
cittamudutā - malleability of consciousness
cittalahutā - lightness of consciousness
citta vīthi - process of consciousness
cittaja-suddhatthaka - inseparable matter produced by consciousness
cittujukatā - rectitude of consciousness
cuti kicca - the death function
cuti citta - death consciousness
cetanā - volition
cetasika - mental factors/phenomena
chanda – desire, will

jaratā - decay
jalābuja - womb-born beings birth
javana - active phase of cognitive process
javana kicca - the function of javana
javana citta - impulsive consciousness
javanavāra - process ending with javana
jāti - birth
jāvitindriya - life-faculty
jīvita-navaka-kalāpa - the group of nine types of matter (vital-nonad)
jīvitasamasīsī - equal cessation with life
jīvhādasaka - the tongue-decad
jīvhā-dvāra-vīthi - the tongue-door cognitive process
jīvhā-viññāna - tongue-consciousness
jīvhā-viññāna-dhātu - tongue-consciousness element
jhāna - meditative absorption

ṭhiti - the presence or existing instant (present development)

tatramajjhattatā - neutrality of mind
tadanuvattika manodvāra - subsequent mind-door process
tadanuvattika manodvāravīthi - conformational mind-door process
tadārammaṇa - registration
tadārammaṇa-vāra - process ends with registration
tadālaṃbana - retentive moment, lit. having that object
tihetuka-puggala - triple-rooted individual
thina - sloth

dassanādi kicca - the function of seeing
diṭṭhi - wrong view
dibba-cakkhu - the divine eye
dibbasota abhiññā - the divine ear
dukkha - unpleasant feeling
duggati-ahetuka-puggala - woeful plane rootless individual
duhetuka-puggala - double-rooted individual
domanassa - displeasure
dosa - hatred
dvāra - door

dhātu - elements

natthi kiñci - nothing whatsoever
nānābaddha avikopana - resolving non-danger to other property
nāmagāhikā - process discerning the name
nāmaggahaṇa vīthi - the process discerning the name of an object
nāmasallakkhaṇā - a process runs recognizing the name
nikanti - mild attachment
nipphanna rūpa - concretely produced matter
nibbattita – abstract
nibbāna - the final bliss
nirodhasamāpatti - attainment of cessation process

pakiṇṇaka cetasika - occasional mental factors
paccaya - condition
pañcakkhandha - five aggregates
pañcadvārāvajjana - five sense door adverting
pañca-dvāra vīthi - five-door cognitive process
paññatti - ordinary conceptual thought

paññā - wisdom
paṭibhāga-nimitta - counter sign image
paṭisandhi - rebirth-linking
paṭisandhi kicca - the re-birth linking function
paṭisandhi citta - rebirth consciousness
pathavī - earth
pathavī kasiṇa - earth-circle
paracittavijānana - the power of penetrating the minds of others to discern their thoughts.
paramattha - ultimate reality
paramparā - sense of process
parikappanā - products of mental construction
parikamma - preliminary
parikamma-nimitta - preparatory sign
paritta - slight
parinibbāna - death after the last lifespan of an Arahant
pīti - joy or zest
puggalajjhāsaya - personal wish or inclination
pubbenivāsānussati - the power to remember one's former existences and the former worlds in which one has lived.
pumbhāvadasaka - the material quality of masculinity
peta - hungry ghost

phala - fruit, fruition
phalasamāpatti vīthi - the path process
phassa - contact

bhanga - cessation or dissolution
bhava - becoming or process of existence
bhava-nikantika - existence-craving
bhavanikantika javana - existence-craving javanas
bhavanga - life continuum consciousness (lit. indispensable condition of existence)
bhavanga kicca - the function of life continuum
bhavangacalana - vibrating bhavanga
bhavangupaccheda - arresting bhavanga
bhūmi - realm or plane of existence or consciousness

magga vīthi - the path process
macchariya - avarice
Majjhima-bhāṇaka - the Middle Sayings

manasikāra - attention
mano-dvāra-vīthi - the mind-door cognitive process
manodvārāvajjana - door adverting consciousness
mano-dhātu - mind-element
mano-viññāna - mind-consciousness
mano-viññāna-dhātu - mind-consciousness element
mahaggata - sublime
mahaggata-vipāka - sublime resultant
mahanta - great
mahābhūta - the great essentials
māna - conceit
middha - torpor
muditā - sympathetic joy
mūla - root
moghavāra - futile course
moha - delusion

yathākammūpaga ñāṇa - the power of seeing beings in the 31 planes of existence and knowing their respective kammas, which have given rise to their rebirths
yamaka-pāṭihāriya - Buddha's twin miracles
yāna - vehicle
yoniso manasikāra - wise attention

rasa - taste; function
rūpa - matter, material phenomenon; fine-material (sphere or plane); visible form
rūpākalāpas - material groups
rūpāvacara vipāka - fine-material-sphere resultants

lahutādi ekādasaka - the undecad of mutability
lobha - greed

vacīviññatti-sadda-navaka - the vocal intimation decad
vacīviññatti-sadda-lahutādi-terasaka - the tri-decad of mutability
vaṇṇa - colour
vaṇṇasallakkhaṇā - recognizing the colour
vatthu - physical base
vatthugāhikā - discerning the entity
vatthusallakkhaṇā - recognizing the entity
vāra - occasion
vicāra - sustained application
vicikicchā - doubt
vicikicchā citta - consciousness accompanied by doubt

viññattigahāna vīthi - intimation comprehending process
viññāna - consciousness
viññāna-dhātu - consciousness elements
vitakka - initial application
vinicchayaggahaṇa vīthi - decision mind-door process
vipassanā - insight or understanding
vipassanā yāna - insight vehicle
vipassanā-yānika - the practise of bare Vipassanā as the vehicle
vibhūta - clear (object)
viratī - abstinences
vīriya - effort, energy
vīthi - process (lit. a way or street)
vedanā - feeling
vehapphala - fourth jhāna realm of Great Reward
voṭṭhabbana - determining (the object)
voṭṭhabbanavāra - a course ending with determining
vodāna - purification, cleansing
vohāra - conventional modes of expression

saṁsedaja - moisture-born beings birth
saññā - perception
sati - mindfulness
saddanavaka - the sound-nonad
saddalahutādi dvādasaka - the dodecad of sound and mutability
saddhā - faith
satthupakkosana - the Buddha's summons
sanketaggahaṇa vīthi - process of taking a recognised sign as the object
sangaha - compendium; combination, inclusion
sangha paṭimānana – Sangha's waiting
santīraṇa - investigating
samatha - concentration or tranquillity
samatha yāna - calm vehicle
samatha-yānika - practise of tranquillity meditation as the vehicle before Vipassanā
samādhi - concentration
samāpajjana - jhānic absorption
samāpajjana vīthi - jhānic process
samudaya - origin (as noble truth)
samudayagāhikā - discerning the object as a whole
samūhaggahaṇa vīthi - the

process discerning the object as a whole
sampaṭicchana - receiving consciousness
sampaṭicchanādi kicca - function of receiving
sambandhaggahaṇa vīthi - the connection between the recognized sign and sound process
sammasana rūpa - matter to be comprehended by insight
sammasitajjhāna - comprehended or investigated jhāna
sammā-ājīva - right livelihood
sammākammanta - right action
sammāvācā - right speech
sammuti - conventional reality
sabhāva - intrinsic nature
sabhāva rūpa - matter possessing intrinsic nature
salakkhaṇarūpa - matter possessing real characteristics
sasankhārika - prompted (consciousnesses)
sādhāraṇa - universal, common
sīla - morality
sukkhavipassaka - practitioners of bare insight
sukha - pleasant feeling
sugati-ahetuka-puggala - blissful plane rootless individual
suddha-manodvāra-vīthi - bare mind-door process
subhakiṇha - realm of Steady Aura
sotadasaka - the ear-decad
sota-dvāra-vīthi - ear-door cognitive process
sota-vatthu - ear-base
sota-viññāna - ear-consciousness
sota-viññāna-dhātu - ear-consciousness element
sobhana - beautiful
sobhana cetasika - beautiful mental factors
sobhana-sādhāraṇa - universal beautiful factors
somanassa - joy
hadayadasaka - heart-decad
hirī - shame
hetu - root or roots

INDEX

Abhidhamma III, VII, IX, XI, 1-7, 9-12, 18, 23-5, 28-9, 34, 36, 38, 41, 44, 47, 58, 62, 69, 73, 75-6, 80-2, 85, 93, 115, 120, 123-4, 129-31, 136
abstinences (viratī) 19
abstract (nibbattita) 10
access (upacāra) 86, 87, 88, 93, 97, 98, 101, 121
acquired or learning sign (uggaha-nimitta) 89
arising instant (uppāda) 36-8
arresting bhavanga (bhavangupaccheda) 27, 42-4, 49, 52, 66, 68, 87, 98, 114, 152, 158
attention (manasikāra) 18
avarice (macchariya) 19

bare mind-door process (suddha-manodvāra-vīthi) 68
bases [twelve] (āyatana) 11
beautiful mental factors (sobhana cetasika) 18-9
becoming or process of existence (bhava) 25, 117
beings having a spontaneous birth (opapātika) 135
bhavanga citta/consciousness 25-6, 30, 41-2, 48-52, 55, 57, 60-2, 66-8, 70-1, 75, 78, 93-5, 101, 104-5, 114-7, 119, 123-5, 135-7
birth (jāti) 14, 131
blissful plane rootless individual (sugati-ahetuka-puggala) 63
bodily intimation-nonad (kāyaviññatti-navaka) 133
body (touching) consciousness 23, 27 30, 32, 35, 39-40, 46
body base (kāya-vatthu) 39
body consciousness (kāya-viññāna) 39
body consciousness element (kāya-viññāna-dhātu) 35
body-decad (kāyadasaka) 132
body-door cognitive process (kāya-dvāra-vīthi) 40-1
Buddha's summons (satthupakkosana) 110-1
Buddha's twin miracles (yamaka-pāṭihāriya) 28

calm vehicle (samatha yāna) 14
cause (kāraṇa) 24
causeless (ahetuka) 28
cessation or dissolution (bhanga) 36, 37, 38
change of lineage (gotrabhū)

moderately desirable (iṭṭhamajjhatta) 46
moisture-born beings birth (saṁsedaja) 135
moment of consciousness (cittakkhaṇa) 38-9
morality (sīla) 3

neighbourhood concentration (upacāra samādhi) 90
neither unpleasant nor pleasant feeling (adukkha-masukha) 22
neutral feeling (upekkhā) 22-3, 88
neutrality of mind (tatramajjhattatā) 19
nibbāna 11, 31, 33, 72-3, 75-7, 97, 99-104, 109, 116, 124-5
noble one (ariya) 99
non-concretely produced matter (anipphanna rūpa) 69, 113, 131
non-delusion (amoha) 24
non-greed (alobha) 19, 24
non-hatred (adosa) 19, 24
nose-base (ghāṇa-vatthu) 39
nose-consciousness (ghāṇa-viññāna) 39
nose-consciousness element (ghāṇa-viññāna-dhātu) 34
nose-decad (ghāṇadasaka) 132
nose-door cognitive process (ghāṇa-dvāra-vīthi) 40
nothing whatsoever (natthi kiñci) 91
nutritive essence (ojā) 131

object (ālambana) 31
object is termed "obscure" (avibhūta) 38, 76
object termed "very slight" (atiparitta) 38
occasional mental factors (pakiṇṇaka cetasika) 18
odour (gandha) 131
one-pointedness of mind (ekaggatā) 18, 88
ordinary conceptual thought (paññatti) 9, 11
other (añña) 18

paramatthadīpanī 76, 83, 166
past bhavanga (atīta-bhavanga) 37, 41-2, 44, 48-9, 51-7, 61, 67-8, 70, 72-5, 114, 116, 119, 158
path citta 14, 98, 128
path process (magga vīthi) 97
path process (phalasamāpatti vīthi) 102, 104
perception (saññā) 18
personal wish or inclination (puggalajjhāsaya) 100
physical base (vatthu) 33, 39
pleasant feeling (sukha) 22-3, 88

volition (cetanā) 18

wholesome (kusala) 24, 28
wieldiness of consciousness (cittakammaññatā) 19
wieldiness of the mental body (kāyakammaññatā) 19
wisdom (paññā) 3, 20
wise attention (yoniso manasikāra) 11, 60
woeful-plane rootless individual (duggati-ahetuka-puggala) 63
womb-born beings (gabbhaseyyaka sattā) 135
womb-born beings birth (jalābuja) 135
worry (kukkucca) 19
wrong view (diṭṭhi) 18

ABOUT PARIYATTI

Pariyatti is dedicated to providing affordable access to authentic teachings of the Buddha about the Dhamma theory (*pariyatti*) and practice (*paṭipatti*) of Vipassana meditation. A 501(c)(3) non-profit charitable organization since 2002, Pariyatti is sustained by contributions from individuals who appreciate and want to share the incalculable value of the Dhamma teachings. We invite you to visit *www.pariyatti.org* to learn about our programs, services, and ways to support publishing and other undertakings.

Pariyatti Publishing Imprints

Vipassana Research Publications (focus on Vipassana as taught by S.N. Goenka in the tradition of Sayagyi U Ba Khin)

BPS Pariyatti Editions (selected titles from the Buddhist Publication Society, copublished by Pariyatti in the Americas)

Pariyatti Digital Editions (audio and video titles, including discourses)

Pariyatti Press (classic titles returned to print and inspirational writing by contemporary authors)

Pariyatti enriches the world by

- disseminating the words of the Buddha,
- providing sustenance for the seeker's journey,
- illuminating the meditator's path.